Cook as the Romans Do

MYRA WALDO

COOK

AS THE ROMANS DO

**Recipies of Rome
and Northern Italy**

COLLIER BOOKS
NEW YORK, N.Y.

A Collier Books Original

First Edition 1961

Collier Books is a division of The Crowell-Collier Publishing Company

Library of Congress Catalog Card Number: 61-18575

Copyright © 1961 by Myra Waldo Schwartz
All Rights Reserved
Hecho en los E.E.U.U.
Printed in the United States of America

Contents

1	The Food, Wine, and Cheese of Northern Italy	9
2	Appetizers	32
3	Soup	38
4	Fish	49
5	Eggs and Cheese	59
6	Pastas and Sauces	65
7	Poultry	85
8	Meats	99
9	Vegetables	129
10	Salads	141
11	Desserts	143
	Index	155

Cook as the Romans Do

Chapter 1

The Food, Wine, and Cheese of Northern Italy

A GREAT MANY Americans think of all Italian food in terms of spaghetti, pizza, and Chianti. Almost automatically, they lump together the entire world of Italian cuisine, believing everything to be doused with tomato sauce and laden with garlic.

This confusion and lack of knowledge about Italy and things Italian is abating somewhat, for Americans are great travelers, and thousands of them have been wandering through every corner of Italy during the past decade or so. To their surprise, they have discovered a tremendous variation in the food styles of the many provinces of Italy, so that a distance of only a hundred miles often brings them into an entirely different culinary area. In Florence, a traveler may dine with pleasure upon a *bistecca alla Fiorentina,* a large juicy cut of steak rubbed with oil and broiled over a wood or charcoal fire. The following day, if he drives his rented car to the northwest and into the ancient harbor city of Genoa, a request for a *bistecca* will fall upon deaf ears. (They can't get a *bistecca* and wouldn't know how to prepare it.) The diner will be urged instead to try the local specialties—*fritto del mare* (fried seafood) or a *zuppa di pesce* (a colorful fish soup). So quickly does the culinary style shift in Italy, that even a half day's run over the lovely countryside brings one to a town with a completely different set of dishes.

But then, why do most Americans think in terms of clichés about Italian food—or about Italians themselves for that matter? Why do they believe that all Italians are dark-haired with swarthy complexions, full of the love of life, very excitable, and always singing a *bel canto* goodbye to their beloved Sorrento or Napoli? They cannot conceive of the fact that the cha-cha-cha is more popular in Rome than the tarantella, although in truth it is. Apparently it is easier for most people to think in simple, general terms, even though these are inevitably wrong. Similarly, in the minds of many Europeans, all Americans are alike; the standardized European caricature of an American is a man wearing a Hawaiian shirt, smoking a long cigar, and living exclusively upon canned or frozen foods. The misunderstanding is mutual, for just as Americans are many different people, physically and mentally, with widely differing interests, so the Italians are many people with equally differing interests. Physically, too, Italians may be short and swarthy, or tall and blond; they may be excitable, but they are just as likely to be calm and placid as an equivalent group of Americans.

How then, did this gross misunderstanding about the cuisine of Italy become a part of American folklore? It appears that about the turn of the century, conditions in southern Italy and Sicily were desperate, and poverty was ever present. Many of the more aggressive and resourceful Sicilians and Neapolitans left their poor homelands to seek their fortunes in the New World. In those days, third-class accommodations, then called by the unappealing name of "steerage," could be had from Italy to America for as little as twenty dollars, and countless thousands of Italians packed a basket filled with food donated by their relatives (meals were not provided aboard ship at that price) and set sail for the continent discovered by their compatriot.

The streets of the New World, they found, were not paved with gold, and they turned to a wide variety of occupations. Among their new endeavors were a series of restaurants specializing in Italian food, and of course they cooked in the style to which they were accustomed, that is, in the manner of southern Italy. Their culinary style was dictated by the cook in the kitchen, often the proprietor's wife, who prepared the very same dishes she had once learned from her mother. The Neapolitan and Sicilian food was good and appetizing and wholesome, and the Americans took to it immediately, so that even the smallest American town soon had its "Italian" restaurant where the American family could gather for a "real Italian meal," consisting of an antipasto, spaghetti with meatballs, and biscuit tortoni. It might be possible to order a meal such as this in a restaurant in Italy, but the odds are against it. Worse still are the impressions which Americans have taken away from the so-called "Italian-American" restaurants, which, in their efforts to compromise two different cuisines, have produced a bland, tasteless style in which nothing seems quite right. For comparison, it is as if an Italian in Hong Kong were to open a restaurant specializing in "Italian-Chinese" cuisine!

The immigrants from southern Italy a little over a half century ago made their mark in many areas of American life, but nowhere more than in gastronomy. Italian dishes became widely and favorably known and unanimously accepted, with every American learning the meaning of Italian food terms such as macaroni, spumoni, ravioli, spaghetti, pizza, and dozens of others. But for the most part, these terms are from the southern half of the country, because very few immigrants came here from the more prosperous north of Italy. Only a small percentage of Americans, therefore, have any idea of the wide scope of northern Italian cuisine, and rare indeed is an American tourist who knows at first sight the meaning of northern Italian food terms such as *gnocchi, fonduta, melanzane alla Parmigiana, fegato Veneziana* and other dishes so characteristic of the north.

It may come as a great surprise to many Americans to learn that spaghetti and macaroni dishes are not very popular in the north, although they constitute the mainstay of the diet in southern Italy. From Naples down to Sicily, *pasta ascuitta,* the wide variety of spaghetti dishes, are the basic and preferred food of everyone, and no meal would be complete without *pasta*. The choice in northern Italy would probably not be for a *pasta,* but rather for a *polenta* (cornmeal) or *risotto* (rice) dish. In any one of the great cities of the north (like Venice, Milan, or Genoa), garlic is not an automatically used ingredient; there are thousands of homes and restaurants in the north where garlic is not frequently used. A great deal more garlic is used, for example, in southern France, in Provence, and the Côte d'Azur, than in northern Italy. In searching about for traditional dishes of the north made with garlic, out of the many thousands of dishes prepared, only a meager few come readily to mind. First, there is the famous *pesto,* a meatless sauce served on a variety of foods in Genoa; there is also the *bagna cauda* sauce of Turin, a hot anchovy dip, into which the diner scoops up the garlic-flavored sauce with raw vegetables. In the beautiful lakes region of Lombardy, on occasion they like to serve a huge rice dish with a *gremolada* sauce, made of herbs and garlic. Around Venice the seafood is a marvel of delicacy, and only rarely is garlic introduced into the local cookery lest it spoil the flavor of the fresh seafood; the only Venetian exception that comes to mind is *baccalà mantecato,* but this is not made with fresh fish, but rather with dried codfish mashed to a paste with garlic. To the east of Venice in the picturesque harbor of Trieste, they make a hearty soup called *iota Triestina,* from beans, potatoes, and sauerkraut with a strong garlic flavor. But these recipes (as well as several others described in this book) are exceptional. Not more than one-tenth of one per cent of north Italian dishes have even a trace of garlic.

Tomatoes, too, are something that the average cook in the north finds useful but not necessarily indispensable. There are innumerable dishes made in the north where tomatoes play no part; one might eat for days around Turin, Florence, Perugia, and Pisa without encountering a single dish containing them. But further to the south in the vicinity of Naples, Sorrento, and Salerno, the cook would throw up his hands in despair if his beloved tomatoes were unavailable! What would become of his sauces for *pasta*, the fish soups, the many dishes flavored with tomatoes?

Not only is north Italian food clearly distinguishable from that of the south, but even within northern Italy, the food styles change suddenly from one district to another, so that many dishes are completely unobtainable a short distance away. It is difficult to understand why a nation should have such varying culinary styles within its borders. Some explanation would seem in order.

First and foremost, it should be recalled that much of Italy became a unified country as recently as 1861; prior to that time, for more than a dozen centuries, local rulers controlled various small districts. A few years later, in 1866, Venice became a part of the Kingdom of Italy, and when the French troops finally withdrew from Rome in 1870, the country was unified—much as we know it today. Only about a century, then, has passed since the unification of the various Italian territories into one nation. During the long period prior to the unification, communication between the various districts was limited (indeed, they were often at war with one another), and local culinary styles developed within small areas without being modified by neighboring regions. Even today, a carryover from previous years of distrust, many provincial Italians regard the people from other parts of their own country with a degree of suspicion, looking upon them as "foreigners." That is not to say that there was not then, nor is not now, a general culinary style in Italy. Of course, certain dishes were popular over larger regions, as for example the *risotto,* the classic rice dish, which was popular all through northern Italy, but its preparation varied a great deal from one section to another. If one orders the dish in Turin it will come with a meat sauce and white truffles; in Milan, the rice will be cooked with chicken stock, white wine, saffron, and onions; in Padua, the *risotto* will be prepared with chicken livers, gizzards and veal; and in Venice, it will be filled with delicious shellfish.

This book concerns itself with some of the outstanding dishes of the northern section of the country. Just as it might be somewhat difficult to define arbitrarily what constitutes the northern half of the United States, so it is with Italy. However, imagine a line drawn across Italy to the northeast, passing through Rome to the Adriatic coast. Everything above will be considered northern, everything below, southern. The province of Latium, in which Rome itself is located, will also be regarded as in the northern part of Italy, mainly because its cuisine is northern. The northern half of the country contains more than a dozen important districts, each with its own distinctive personality and culinary styles. As many specialties as possible have been included in this book in order to offer a broad sampling of the northern cuisine. But we have avoided those dishes, the ingredients of which are unavailable to the American cook, and/or those which might be confusing to anyone unacquainted with the complexities of north Italian cookery. Visitors to the ancient seaport of Trieste, for instance, would surely want to have *brodetto di pesce,* a marvelous seafood soup, but they could not make is successfully at home, because the dish requires Adriatic fish. In the province of Venetia, which includes the city of Venice, culinary ingenuity reaches great heights. There are numerous seafood soups, dishes involving tiny clams and miniature octopus (which taste like fried clams), plus such staples of Italian cuisine as *risi e bisi* (rice and peas), *fegato alla Veneziana* (liver cut into thin strips and sautéed with onions and white wine). *Manzo alla Veneziana* is beef prepared with onions and white wine in a casserole. Another popular Venetian dish is homely cornmeal, yellow or white, eaten plain or cut into slices and fried, or served with small game birds and occasionally as *polenta pastizada,* that is, slices of firm polenta, intermixed with a chicken liver, tomato, and vegetable sauce.

Around the almost Austrian city of Bolzano, in the extreme north near the Austrian frontier, *gnocchi* are in great favor, sometimes filled with chopped sausage, liver, spinach or almost anything the cook has available. One of the big specialties is *ravioli alla Trentina,* little envelopes of dough stuffed with onions, chicken, and meat, all ground to a fine paste. *Frittata Trentina* is something like a pancake and is served with a sauce of onions, cheese, and mushrooms.

Lombardy, with Milan as its center, cooks with butter rather than with oil, and so at first encounter its cuisine often seems more French than Italian. Lombardy has contributed many dishes to the classic cuisine of the world —even the French have adopted many of them. It was here that *minestrone,* that delightful thick soup of vegetables and *pasta* first began. As I mentioned previously, *risotto* is prepared a dozen or more ways in northern Italy, but *alla Milanese* has become a standard recipe, prepared with white wine and onions and colored with saffron. *Occi Buci,* veal shanks, may or may not be an original Milanese dish (as the Milanese claim), but surely no one can dispute *costoletta alla Milanese,* the lightly breaded veal chop which has become standard restaurant fare the world over.

The chief city of the Piedmont district is Turin, an industrial giant. It is surprising to find completely rural countryside just a few miles out of this sophisticated metropolis. City and country are responsible for two different cookery styles within the Piedmont: one, complex and urban, the other, simple and rural, but very delicious nonetheless. In the city, there is butter cookery in the French style, a cuisine which seems imitative of both Switzerland and France. But the district holds such culinary riches as *agnolotti* (which are like ravioli, only much larger), the *fonduta* (a melted cheese dish made with the distinctive Fontina cheese), and the *bagna cauda* sauce. In the Piedmont countryside, the curious traveler who is fortunate enough to locate a quiet country inn may eat *polenta,* the classic corn meal dish prepared in a dozen different fashions—with buckwheat, anchovies and cheese, or possibly baked with layers of Fontina cheese, or a sweet *polenta* made with vanilla flavoring and sugar.

American tourists frequently enter Italy by way of the coast road, driving over from Nice and the French Riviera into Liguria, whose coast is called the Italian Riviera. Bustling Genoa is the heart of this region. Many Ligurian dishes are, naturally, based upon seafood, for this province lies along the blue Mediterranean Sea. But the one basic item that flavors Ligurian food is *il pesto,* the classic flavoring sauce of Genoa; this remarkable concoction is made of basil, pine nuts, olive oil, cheese, and garlic, all finely ground. It has a remarkably pungent, but appetizing aroma and taste. The Genoese put it in soups and almost everything else; however, it finds its greatest uses in sauces served with a variety of *pastas*. Incidentally, ravioli and *trenette* (thin noodles) reach great heights of culinary excellence with *pesto* sauce.

Emilia-Romagna includes the city of Bologna, twice renowned—for its great university founded in the fifth century and for its marvelous cookery, *alla Bolognese*—to most Italians, the best and most delicious (and incidentally, the most fattening) food of all Italy. Many hungry tourists would place Bolognese cookery above the intellectual distinction of the city. To wander about the arched streets of this ancient town is an absolute gastronomic delight; nowhere else in the world are there such delightful arrangements of food. The vegetables are scrubbed clean and placed in colorful array, the fruits are marvels of perfection, baskets of berries are displayed artistically with pleasing symmetry. The windows are decorated with *pasta* in a bewildering assortment—the mind cannot cope with dozens upon dozens of different shapes of *pasta* from the tiniest, no larger than a grain, to enormous tubelike shapes into which one might conceivably place an arm. The *pasta* comes in imaginative forms, some fashioned like bows, others like hats; there are star shapes, ribbons, curls, spirals, abstract designs, rounded elbows, and so on until one's memory fails. From the ceiling, the food merchant hangs his sausages, the enormous hams, the dried and salted meats, and the classic *mortadella* sausage, the one which food-conscious citizens and visiting gourmets acclaim. Bologna, in particular, and some parts of Emilia and Romagna love rich food and sauces. The *pastas,* marvels of perfection, including such things as *lesagne verdi* (green noodles), *tagliatelle* (wide egg noodles), *capelletti* and *tortellini* (two types of *pasta* which are customarily stuffed with delicious mixtures), but perhaps best of all are the simple *pappardelle,* flat noodles. If a dish is marked *alla Bolognese,* it frequently indicates a rich meat sauce, locally called *ragu.*

The bountiful province of Tuscany, lying northwest of Rome and famous for its cities of Florence and Pisa crammed with centuries of lively history, is a particular favorite with visitors from America; here are the fascinating cities of Florence, Pisa, and Siena, with the wonderful food which may be found in this region. If there is one single item which the Tuscans love above all others, it is the humble bean, and *alla Toscana* (in the style of Tuscany) often means the dish contains beans. But of course Tuscany food is complicated; beans are not necessarily the beginning and end of the provincial cuisine. However, before leaving beans, special note should be taken of the favorite dish called *fagioli all'Uccelletto,* sage-flavored beans cooked with olive oil and covered with tomato sauce. The *cacciucco,* a delicious fish soup-stew, is also classic in this region. In and around the noble city of Florence, the *bistecca alla Fiorentina* is, as I mentioned before, a thick cut of steak wiped with oil and charcoal broiled. The Florentines also do well with vegetables, particularly asparagus *alla Fiorentina* (with butter, cheese, and eggs), broccoli *alla Fiorentina* (with oil and garlic), and especially with artichokes, which they make up as an omelet, or with a cream and cheese sauce. *Trippa alla Fiorentina,* if you like tripe, is possibly the best tripe dish in the world.

The Marches, that coastal region lying along the Adriatic, to the north and east of Rome, is somewhat out of the regular tourist beat. The Italians come here for their summer vacations, to enjoy their beaches and to eat the good food of the region. The *brodettos* are marvelous along the coast—fish soups made with all sorts of Adriatic denizens of the deep, but the recipes vary widely from cook to cook; sometimes the *brodetto* is as thick as a *bouillabaisse* prepared in Marseille, sometimes it is clear and almost like a clam broth. The *lasagne* in the Marches is marvelously satisfying, being filled with cream, ham, truffles, and mushrooms.

Umbria embraces that quartet of highlights for tourists —Perugia, Assisi, Orvieto, and Spoleto. The people are particularly fond of game, especially wild pigeons or doves. The sausages are excellent here, although it is perhaps better to eat them before one learns (to one's dismay!) their somewhat exotic contents. Truffles, those mysterious mushroom-tubers, are very popular, particularly the *tartufi neri,* or black truffles, which are used in many dishes, but are best of all in spaghetti sauces. Desserts are good here, for in all of northern Italy, it is only in Umbria that cakes and sweets are so popular.

Latium is the province that incorporates the eternal city of Rome. Naturally, all the best Italian cooking may be found here, although southern-style Neapolitan and Sicilian cooking is apt to be considered with condescension. One of the greatest specialties of Latium is *abbacchio,* baby lamb so small that the diner is often served a dozen tiny chops as a portion. *Abbacchio* is prepared in a wide variety of styles, but in the opinion of many *alla cacciatora* cooked with anchovies and vinegar, is the best of all. *Alla Romana* is delicious, too, prepared with white wine. The Romans love spaghetti and its variants; *fettucine alla Romana* are noodles at their best, rich and satisfying with butter, cream, and grated cheese. *Spaghetti all'Amatriciana* has a tomato, onion, and pork sauce; *alla Carbonara* is made with chopped bits of bacon and uncooked egg and is absolutely delicious. The *stufatino alla Romana* is a beef stew, admittedly, but the Romans make it very well indeed with red wine, onions, and bacon. The favorite vegetable of the Romans is probably the artichoke, prepared in many styles, but *alla Romana,* with parsley, olive oil, and white wine is hard to beat.

The wines of Italy are almost a necessity for the full enjoyment of Italian food. Somehow, in its own way, nature has managed to see to it that Italian wines have the ideal qualities required to accompany Italian food; some magical combination of grapes, climate, and soil produces a whole series of wines which seem predestined to be served with Italian food. A chianti, for example, perfect with Italian food, would be completely unsuitable with French food. No matter how delicious a glorious dish of *pasta* may be, it is incomplete without a glass of wine, which is not only marvelous in itself but greatly enhances the *pasta*. Most Italians would scarcely consider a meal without wine, and a good number might actually refuse to eat food unaccompanied by wine.

Many people, particularly those inclined to be snobbish about wines, automatically assume that Italian wine means the cheap, cloudy red type poured out of a pitcher in a family-style Italian restaurant in Kansas City, Missouri. The more sophisticated know something about a few Italian wines. They have learned that wine out of an Italian bottle is inevitably better than wine from a carafe or pitcher. But comparatively few have learned about the wonderful wines that are produced in the north. It is a pleasure to report that Italian wines are rarely expensive, usually selling for two dollars a bottle or less in the United States; a more expensive bottle (except for a sparkling wine) is a comparative rarity.

Italian wines are, as a rule, either red or white. Although in the past few years the American vogue for *rosé,* or pink wine, has created a supply, the *rosés* are in the minority. The average Italian does not particularly care for *rosé;* he much prefers a red or white wine with his meals. Unlike Frenchmen, the vast majority of Italians make little or no fuss about vintages—what wine is ideal with what food—but merely enjoy wine as they would enjoy the company of a good friend, or the pleasure of sunshine. To the

Italian, wine is inseparable from food, and he makes no more fuss about it than he might about bread, although he knows good wine from bad by instinct. But, of course, like wine drinkers the world over, he follows a general rule or two, although these are simple indeed. With fish, Italians like a dry white wine, and this, too, they drink with *antipasto,* or spaghetti, or macaroni dishes prepared with a fish sauce. With red meats and poultry, they usually prefer a dry red wine. (A dry wine, of course, is merely one which is not sweet.) Also, in the general tradition of wine-drinking the world over, white wine is served cooled or chilled, whereas red wine is preferred at room temperature. Sweet and sparkling wines are rarely served with food; in general these specialty wines are reserved for evening refreshment or for parties.

Wines in Italy are somewhat less exactingly prepared than they are in France, where standards are more carefully checked by the wine associations. In Bordeaux and Burgundy, the wine-makers are carefully regulated and subject to control by various government agencies, but in Italy, although there are wine laws which are headed in the right direction, the wines are quite likely to vary in quality. Frequently, two bottles bearing identical markings and from the same bottler will taste quite differently. This is seldom the result of a desire to defraud the public but rather an example of the happy-go-lucky attitude of some Italian wine-makers. One finds the criticism of Italian wine disappearing as wine-making in Italy becomes more scientific. Of course, it should be remembered that wine is grown in every single province, from the northern borders touching Austria to the southernmost parts of Sicily, and it is rare to find a farmer who does not make wine at least for his own use. Naturally, wines produced in local areas vary according to the temperament and ability of the farmers; but the improvement in Italian wines has reference chiefly to large-scale operations of commercial vineyards which ship not only to the local markets but also to the United States.

Wine is made everywhere in Italy, but certain types

have become established, classic in that they have been recognized for their distinction, and their names of origin protected by the Italian government. The Italians, it should be pointed out, separate red "table" wines, which are of lesser quality, from "roast" wines (suitable for serving with roast meats), which they consider of higher quality.

Beginning in the north with the Piedmont district, there is a tremendous variety and range of wines shipped to the market. In no particular order of excellence, there are such important wines as the following: Barolo, a very smooth dry red wine, classified as a roast wine. Barbaresco is similar to Barolo but may be somewhat smoother. Barbera is rather higher in alcoholic content, and although regarded as a table wine when young, it is considered a roast wine when mature. Freisa d'Asti is lower in alcoholic content than Barbera, somewhat crude and rough when young, but softer and better when mature. Gattinara has a wonderful color and a marvelous "raspberry" flavor; many connoisseurs regard this wine as just about the best of all Italian wines. Grignolino d'Asti has a brilliant red color and comes in both dry and sweet types, but the dry is far better. Nebbiolo Piedmontese is classified only as a table wine when young, but a roast wine when several years old. Brachetto d'Asti has very little alcohol and is fairly sweet; it is best when served as a dessert wine. Cortese dell'Alto is a light white wine with a pleasing bouquet. Monferrato is straw-colored but has a greenish undertone; it is only good when young. Carema is a red wine which is rarely encountered; it is crude and rough when young, but it improves greatly with maturity. Dolcetto delle Langhe is also quite rare, but it has a good bouquet accompanied by a slightly bitter taste. Moscato d'Asti has little alcohol, but the taste is distinctively that of a sweet Muscat grape. Also made in the Piedmont district is Asti Spumante (sometimes just called Asti), the standard Italian sparkling wine; it is not too bad, but is quite sweet.

In Liguria, which encompasses the Italian Riviera, the wines are not quite so good, but passable nonetheless. Unfortunately, not too many Ligurian wines are exported to the United States and are therefore not easily encountered except on a trip to Italy. Cinque Terre may be found occasionally in this country in Italian wine shops; it is a pale white wine, somewhat aromatic with a fair flavor. It comes in dry or sweet styles, but the sweet wine is somewhat tiresome and lacking in subtlety; this type is usually marked Giacomelli Schiachetra. Vermentino Ligure is a yellow-green wine, with a dry, somewhat prickly quality, and a noticeably strong bouquet. Coronata, made just outside of Genoa, is a dry white wine with a golden cast, of only average quality. The best red wine of Liguria is probably from the region of Dolceacqua, which sells its wines chiefly as Rossese, a dry red wine of quite good quality. Polcevera is a white wine available in two styles, dry or sweet; it is only moderately good. Bianco di Portofino is a fruity, vaguely sparkling white wine which is pleasant when it is drunk in that lovely fishing village, but considerably less impressive elsewhere.

Compared to those of Piedmont or Venetia, the wines of Lombardy (Milano and the lakes region) are secondary. Around the shores of Lake Garda, a charming region, are grown the various light red and *rosé* wines which are becoming so popular; these are sold under various names, including Chiaretto, Garda, or Riviera del Garda. Sassella may be the best wine of Lombardy; it is a bright ruby-red color with an interesting taste and qualifies as a roast wine when aged. Grumello is quite similar to Sassella, but many find it one step beneath that wine in quality. Inferno is another wine in the same general category as Sassella and Grumello, but Inferno, too, is somewhat beneath Sassella. Valgella is a little milder in taste, and with a lesser bouquet than any of the Lombardy wines previously mentioned; it is seldom exported. Some red and white wines, under the generic name of Valtellina, are produced around the Swiss border but are generally considered unimportant. A sparkling wine, Moscato di Casteggio, is sweet and just slightly sticky to the palate; it has a strong bouquet.

Around the mountain resort city of Bolzano (the region

nearest Austria), there are no really important wines, but several are quite interesting. There is Santa Maddalena, a ruby-red wine with a fair degree of excellence; it has a pleasing aroma and a delicate taste. Caldaro comes in several varieties (like Schiave and Rossara, for example); it is somewhat ordinary when young, but when mature develops into a fine red roast wine. Terlano is a white wine with a yellow-green cast; it has a quite dry, aromatic quality. Termeno comes in dry and slightly sweet types, with an undertone of bitterness, but it is quite smooth nevertheless. Meranese di Collina is not remarkable; it is a dry, light red wine which seldom matures with distinction. Guncinà and Santa Guistina are two other red wines commonly encountered only in the mountain inns surrounding Bolzano and the general vicinity. Marzemino is a light ruby color, slightly acid in taste, and never completely dry. A favorite violet-colored wine with a uniquely tart flavor said to resemble that of raspberries, is Teroldego; it may mature into a superior roast wine. Val d'Aldige, which matures in the same way, is a dry red wine of somewhat low alcoholic content. Lagrein Rosato is the only worthwhile *rosé* wine of this district.

Euganean Venetia covers the district to the west and north of Venice; from here come three of the leading wines of Italy, as well as several others entitled to be regarded as close contenders. The vineyards around Verona are world famous with connoisseurs of Italian wines, but all through Euganean Venetia there are scores of excellent vineyards. Soave is a straw-colored wine with a slightly greenish tinge; many experts claim that of all Italian white wines, Soave is closest to a French Chablis, which automatically enhances its importance. Valpolicella is surely one of the very best red wines of Italy, if not the best, as many Veronese claim. It is extremely smooth, quite reliable from bottle to bottle (in and of itself exceptional for an Italian wine) and very well balanced; this wine, too, has often been compared to a French claret, perhaps more often than any other Italian red wine. When aged for five years or so, Valpolicella matures perfectly and becomes one of the best roast wines of all. From an adjacent valley come Valpanena, which is almost but not quite as good as the original Valpolicella, but otherwise it is quite similar. The third great wine of this district is Bardolino, grown along the southeast shores of Lake Garda. It is a brilliantly clear, ruby-red wine, sometimes with a slightly prickly taste; it is neither a subtle nor a complex wine, but it is almost ideal with a plate of spaghetti or any other hearty, appetizing fare.

Although scarcely in the same category with the reds, some of the white wines of Venetia are worthy of mention. Colli Euganei is pleasant and light, with a good taste; Verdiso is possibly even better, with a lovely golden color. Garganega di Gambellara is straw-colored; its light and delicate bouquet makes it ideal with fish dishes. Prosecco di Conegliano is a bright yellow in color with a slightly prickling taste; the still wine is fairly good, but it is also made up into a tiresome and sticky, sweet, sparkling wine. As a novelty, and only as that, there is the sweet red dessert wine called Recioto Veronese; it is best taken as refreshment between meals, because it does not go too well with food. A generic term, Vino Veronese, is used to describe the typical, routine red wines produced around Verona, and found in the taverns and homes in this area. They are never exported abroad, nor even shipped to the larger cities of Italy.

The region of Emilia-Romagna (Bologna and its surrounding territory) is famous for its marvelous, rich food but not so highly regarded for the wines produced there. Undoubtedly the leading wine is Lambrusco, a red wine with a bright color and a tart taste; it is usually slightly sparkling or prickly. Lambrusco, however, has its critics; many find it a poor sort of wine, lacking in quality. It does seem to accompany the highly seasoned, fatty food of Bologna, however, although it is somewhat less satisfactory with other fare. Sangiovese (di Romagna) is a dry, garnet-colored wine with a bitter flavor; sometimes the biting aftertaste is pleasant, at other times it seems to overpower the wine. Albana (di Romagna) is a white wine, with a rather pleasing golden color. It comes as both a dry wine and a semisweet type.

The outstanding wine of the Marches is Verdicchio (sometimes with the added name of Dei Castelli di Jesi), known for its lovely straw and gold color. It is the sort of white wine which perfectly accompanies any fish dish or hors d'oeuvre, and there are many who find it superior to Soave or Orvieto, but this is a matter of personal taste and opinion; in any event, it is undoubtedly one of the very best Italian dry white wines. On a slightly lower scale is Vernaccia, which is nonetheless a very pleasant wine. Rosso Piceno (or sometimes Piceno Rosso) is a delightful red wine with low alcoholic content, but it has a vaguely bitter aftertaste; it comes both as a dry and also as a semisweet wine.

The lovely district of Tuscany, northwest, is famous for the best known, and possibly the least understood, of all Italian wines, Chianti. Even those American who could not select a French wine from a list would have no hesitation in ordering Chianti at any Italian restaurant. Very likely, Chianti is the best known wine in the world. Without pretensions of any sort—and not to be taken too seriously—it is a wine that has been accepted the world over, but perhaps nowhere so wholeheartedly as in the United States. Much of the Chianti is produced in the region immediately to the south of Florence. So much Chianti is bottled here each year, in fact, that no one knows the exact total, but it seems certain that a vast river of it flows forth to be downed happily by millions of people in Italy and around the globe. Chianti comes in both red and white types, but it is the red which has made the reputation for the wine; the white Chianti is generally mediocre. Red Chianti is dry, with a fine ruby color, but is somewhat crude in taste. Incidentally, the color may vary a good deal depending upon the particular type. A considerable quantity of very ordinary red wine is produced in southern Italy and shipped north for blending with the more popular wines of Tuscany, sad to relate. The ordinary Chianti is shipped in its traditional bottle, more or less squat in shape, enclosed in its *fiasco*, a straw covering which permits the bottle to stand upright. However, the finest Chianti is sold in regular wine bottles and marked *Classico*, and these classic Chiantis are aged until they finally become a truly superb wine, far better than the ordinary straw-covered product.

Very similar to Chianti is Brolio, which is grown nearby and has the same general characteristics; like Chianti, it improves greatly with age. Rufina, too, is quite like Chianti, as is Carmignano (although this wine is somewhat rare, as it is produced in small quantities). Pomino is one step away from Chianti but very similar in its character, and Montalbano is another dry red wine in the same general class. A superior red wine produced around Siena is the ruby-red one called Vin Nobile de Montepulciano, or the Noble Wine of Montepulciano, a high-sounding title indeed.

Tuscany produces other white wines, too, besides the white Chianti. To list them briefly: Montecarlo, Procanico (form Elba), Passiti, and Vin Santo Toscano, this last an outstanding dessert wine. The Spumante d'Elba is a sweet, white, sparkling wine, of no particular character, made on the island of Elba.

Umbria (the region around Perugia) is not too well known for its wine, with the exception of Orvieto, which has made a name for itself. Like Chianti, Orvieto is shipped in a straw *fiasco* and comes in two styles—a dry wine with about 12.5 per cent alcohol, and a rather sweet type with less alcohol. The dry Orvieto is far superior, with an excellent flinty taste remniscent of a Pouilly-Fuissé or a Chablis; it has a delicate flavor accompanied by a vaguely bitter (although not unpleasant) aftertaste. The sweet type can only be used as a dessert wine, for it is somewhat cloying.

In Latium (Rome and surrounding area), the vintners produce some adequate wines, but none is of any degree of excellence. The general name of Castelli Romani is used to describe the wines produced on a series of volcanic hills southeast of Rome; the chief districts are

Frascati, Colonna, Marino, Montecompatri, Velletri, and the Alban and Lanuvian Hills. Of these, all white wines, porbably the best known is Frascati, an extremely popular table wine in all classes of Roman society. Everyone in Rome seems to drink Frascati as a matter of course. All the wines of the Castelli Romani are very pleasant and drinkable, but not outstanding; and since they do not travel well, they are seldom encountered outside of Rome and its suburbs. In Montefiascone, they produce the wine called *Est! Est!! Est!!!* (the exclamation marks are part of the name), a white wine of little distinction, although its name is fascinating. There is a story about this wine: it seems that German cardinal, traveling in Italy, sent his servant ahead with orders to designate suitable places for the Cardinal's refreshment on the walls of wine taverns, using either *Est* (meaning "it is good") or *Non Est* ("it is not good"). The servant became enthralled with this wine and enthusiastically marked *Est! Est!! Est!!!* on the walls for the thirsty cardinal. Unhappily, the wine does not seem nearly so good today.

A light yellow wine produced in this region and called Malvasia di Grottaferrata is quite pleasant, although not otherwise important; the same can be said of the Moscat di Terracina. Acqua del Serino is a dry white wine of passable quality. The reds are little better; Cesane del Piglio has a ruby-red color which is pleasant to behold; it is not too good when young, but much better when older. Aleatico del Viterbese is a sweet red wine with a lovely purple color and a fine bouquet, but it is only suitable with dessert.

Italy is a country of cheeses, many of a high order of excellence. Although the variety is scarcely equal to that of France, where literally hundreds of different types are made, Italian cheeses are almost always very good. Of the scores made in Italy, three have achieved worldwide recognition—Gorgonzola, Bel Paese, and Parmesan. All of these originate in the northern part of the country.

Gorgonzola is one of the three important "blue" cheeses of the world, the other two being Roquefort and English

Stilton. The Italian cheese is made from cow's milk, whereas France's Roquefort is prepared with sheep's milk and, in addition, the blue veining is produced in a different manner. Roquefort, moreover, is very crumbly, whereas Gorgonzola is rich and creamy. Which one of these three Italian cheeses is the best is surely a matter of personal preference. Very much like Gorgonzola is another Italian cheese, Calvenzano, made in Bergamo. Castelmagno is another imitation of Gorgonzola, although not quite so delicious. Dolce Verde, literally "sweet green", is another type of Gorgonzola, as is Erbo; both are quite good, with a pleasing salty taste.

Bel Paese is the classic "mild" cheese of the world, which anyone and everyone can like immediately. It has a creamy yellow butterlike consistency, ideal for eating alone or with fruits, and it may also be used in cooking. Bel Paese comes in a wide variety of sizes and flavors, but all are smooth, unctuous, and mild. Pastorella is a small Bel Paese; Bel Paesino is a fairly good imitation, somewhat smaller, but seeming to lack the full flavor of the original. Fior d'Alpe is a fair copy, but one step below the original in character and taste; Robiola is about the same. However, one variation of Bel Paese seems to have won general acceptance: this is Tallegio, a soft smooth cheese with a slight pungency. Two other types are quite different—Robiolina and Tallegino, both somewhat stronger and more pungent that Bel Paese and therefore not necessarily to everyone's taste.

Parmesan (also called Parmigiano) cheese completes the triumvirate of Italian "greats." When some fresh young Parmesan can be located (and this is not easy, for most of it is sold when aged and firm), it is difficult to imagine a more interesting table cheese. In Italy, Parmesan is familiarly called *grana* and has been made for so long that no one can be sure when it first originated, but it was certainly not less than two thousand years ago. The cheese was originally produced near Parma, from which it of course gets its name; however, it is also being made now in other localities. When made in Lodi (in

Lombardy), it is called *grana Lodigiana;* when produced in Reggio Emilia, the name is *grana Reggiana,* and so on. Any dish in the Italian cuisine which is sprinkled or covered with Parmesan cheese is usually designated as *"alla Parmigiana,"* but this is not always accurate, for many such dishes had their origin elsewhere. (The cuisine of Parma is not nearly so extensive as the great number of dishes called *"alla Parmigiana"* would indicate.) Parmesan, when used for grating, should be at least two years old (it is then called Parmigiano Vecchio); when slightly older it is known as Stravecchio, then subsequently as Stravecchione.

As Parmesan is a rather expensive cheese, and also because success breeds imitations, this great product has been copied frequently. Romano, for example, is a whitish cheese, very like Parmesan. Pecorino, too, is similar, although it is made with sheep's milk. And sometimes one encounters a cheese called Pecorino Romano that is made only in Sardinia. In the Marches district, they make a type of Pecorino from sheep's milk called Bazzotto; another imitation in this category is Emiliano, which is distinguished by a rather sharp, spicy taste.

Speaking of imitations, the Italians prepare a cheese much like the one Americans call Swiss, but which the Swiss people call Emmentaler; this imitation is called Fontina, and it is very pleasant, although quite rich and fatty. Something like Fontina is Battelmatt, smooth and unctuous. Gruviera (sometimes called Groviera) is a direct imitation of Swiss Gruyère, that is, Swiss cheese without holes.

Another important Italian cheese is Ricotta, which is enormously popular in Rome. This is a fresh cheese, much like our own cottage cheese, but much more flavorsome. In Italy, Ricotta is made from unsalted ewe's milk, whereas it is prepared from cow's milk in the United States. When the Italians add salt to Ricotta, it is called Ricotta Salata.

A quick rundown of some of the other lesser cheeses of the north: Asiago is prepared in Lombardy and Venetia;

it is a lightly flavored cheese made with cow's milk. Around Umbria, they make Caciofiore, a pleasing little-known fresh cheese from cow's milk which turns out to be something like soft butter. Another fresh cow's milk cheese is Caciotte, made in the Marches. Certosino is a good, mild cheese, white and pleasing and worthy of more recognition; it is barely known in the United States. Ciclio is a small cream cheese, the sort enjoyed by everyone; another one in this category is Cremini, made in Cremona.

In Lombardy, they prepare a delicious whole milk cheese called Crescenza, with a soft consistency and a mild, sweet flavor; this cheese also occasionally appears as Crescenza Lombardi and Carsenza. Another Lombardy cheese is Mascarpone, a small white cream cheese. From the north, the Val d'Aosta, comes Fior d'Alpe (The Flowers of the Alps), a hard cheese with a tangy taste. In Emilia, they make Formaggio dei Pastori from sheep's milk; it is apt to have quite an unpleasant aroma. Sbrinz is a Lombardy cheese with a distinctive, grainy quality.

Of course, northern Italy produces dozens of other cheeses all worthy of investigation, but difficult to locate except in the particular provinces where they are made. Many cheeses of southern Italy, such as Mozzarella and Provolone, have become popular in the north, but this discussion has limited itself to cheeses which have originated in the northern half of the country.

Any cheese must be treated carefully to bring out its flavor. By all means, avoid "processed" or prepackaged cheeses, and, if possible, buy authentic products from an Italian grocery or food specialty shop in portions weighing about a pound. Wrap your cheeses tightly in Saran wrap so as to exclude the air; store them in the refrigerator. For further protection, wrap aluminum foil around the Saran wrap, or if you prefer, wet a kitchen towel thoroughly, then wring it out, and wrap several folds of moist cloth around the cheese. At least three hours before eating the cheese, remove from the refrigerator, unwrap, and expose to the air so that the cheese can slowly and gradually come to room temperature. However, be sure not to warm cheese artificially in order to bring it to room temperature. Cold cheese, freshly removed from the refrigerator, has very little flavor.

Italian food, Italian wines, Italian cheeses are all delightful. Enjoy them to the full. *Buon appetito!*

Myra Waldo

Chapter 2

Appetizers

BAGNA CAUDA

Hot Anchovy Dip (For Raw Vegetables)

¼ pound butter	½ cup finely chopped
¼ cup olive oil	anchovies
5 cloves garlic, thinly sliced	Crisp, raw vegetables

Combine the butter, oil, and garlic in a small saucepan. Place over very low heat or boiling water for 15 minutes, but do not let the mixture boil. Mix in the anchovies until dissolved. Pour into a small chafing dish to keep warm. Serve surrounded with sliced artichokes, cucumber sticks, celery, endive, cauliflower flowerets, or any crisp raw vegetable.

CROSTINI di FEGATO

Chicken Liver Pâté on Toast

1 pound chicken livers	¼ teaspoon freshly ground
4 tablespoons butter	black pepper
¼ cup finely chopped onion	2 teaspoons drained chopped
½ cup chicken broth	capers
1 teaspoon salt	

Wash the livers, removing any discolored areas and connective tissues. Purée the raw livers in an electric blender or chop very fine.

Melt the butter in a skillet; sauté the onion until yellow and transparent. Add the broth; cook over medium heat 5 minutes. Stir in the livers, salt, and pepper until no pink remains; mix constantly. Remove from heat and add the capers. Chill. Spread on sautéed Italian or French bread.

Serves 6.

CROSTINI di POMODORI

Tomato Canapes

4 tablespoons butter	¼ teaspoon freshly ground black pepper
¾ cup finely chopped onions	¼ cup grated Parmesan cheese
2 cups peeled chopped tomatoes	2 egg yolks, beaten
1 teaspoon salt	2 tablespoons minced parsley
	5 slices toast, cut in half

Melt the butter in a skillet; sauté the onions 10 minutes. Add the tomatoes, salt, and pepper. Cook over low heat 10 minutes or until no liquid remains. Cool. Mix in the cheese, egg yolks, and parsley; taste for seasoning—the mixture should be spicy. Spread on the toast; arrange on a greased baking sheet. Bake in a preheated 400° oven 10 minutes or until lightly browned. Serve immediately.

Makes 10 canapes.

PEPERONI alla Piemontese

Pepper Appetizer

6 green and red peppers	½ cup minced anchovies
1½ cups peeled cubed tomatoes	3 tablespoons dry bread crumbs
3 cloves garlic, sliced	3 tablespoons olive oil
4 tablespoons butter	

Red and green peppers may be used or all green or red. Cut the peppers in quarters lengthwise; scoop out the seeds and fibres.

Mix together the tomatoes, garlic, anchovies, bread crumbs, and oil. Stuff the pepper quarters. Arrange in an oiled baking pan; dot with the butter. Bake in a 375° oven 30 minutes or until crisply tender. Serve cold.

Serves 6.

INSALATA di SCAMPI e FUNGHI

Shrimp and Mushroom Appetizer

1 pound firm white mushrooms	⅛ teaspoon minced garlic
½ cup olive oil	1 pound cooked cleaned shrimp
4 tablespoons lemon juice	1¼ teaspoons salt
½ teaspoon freshly ground black pepper	

2 tablespoons minced parsley

Wash and dry the mushrooms. Remove the stems and use for another purpose. Slice the caps paper thin; add the oil, lemon juice, pepper, and garlic. Marinate in the refrigerator 2 hours, mixing frequently.

Thirty minutes before serving, mix in the shrimp and salt. Taste for seasoning. Sprinkle with the parsley.

Serves 4-6.

ANTIPASTO di FUNGHI e POMODORI

Mushroom and Tomato Appetizer

4 firm tomatoes	3 tablespoons olive oil
1 teaspoon salt	2 tablespoons lemon juice
½ teaspoon freshly ground black pepper	8 large mushrooms, thinly sliced
1 teaspoon minced fresh basil or ⅛ teaspoon, dried	

Peel and slice the tomatoes. Arrange on a serving dish. Season with the salt, pepper, and basil; then sprinkle with half the olive oil and lemon juice. Arrange the sliced mushrooms over them, then sprinkle with the remaining oil and lemon juice.

Serves 6-8.

FAGIOLI TOSCANI col TONNO

Bean and Tuna Fish Appetizer

1½ cup dried white beans	½ cup olive oil
1 clove garlic, split	½ teaspoon freshly ground
2 teaspoons salt	black pepper
½ cup thinly sliced onions	2 7¾-ounce cans tuna fish

Wash the beans, cover with water and bring to a boil; let soak 1 hour. Drain. Add fresh water to cover and the garlic. Bring to a boil and cook over low heat 2 hours or until tender. Add the salt after 1½ hours cooking time. Drain well and discard the garlic.

Toss the beans with the onions (separated into rings), the oil, and pepper. Chill. Drain the tuna and cut into chunks. Arrange on top of the beans.

Serves 6-8.

FAGIOLI con CAVIALE

White Beans and Caviar

2 cups dried white beans	¼ teaspoon freshly ground
2 teaspoons salt	black pepper
¼ cup olive oil	½ cup black caviar

Wash the beans. Cover with water and bring to a boil; let soak 1 hour. Drain. Add fresh water to cover and bring to a boil; cover and cook over low heat 2 hours or until tender. Add the salt after 1 hour of cooking time. Drain.

Toss the beans with the oil and pepper. Mix in the caviar lightly. Serve with lemon wedges.

Serves 6-8.

Note: Danish or Icelandic caviar (much less expensive) may be used in this dish.

FUNGHI alla PARMIGIANA

Cheese-Stuffed Mushrooms

2 pounds mushrooms	3 tablespoons minced parsley
½ cup grated Parmesan cheese	1 teaspoon salt
¾ cup dry bread crumbs	½ teaspoon freshly ground black pepper
½ cup grated onions	½ teaspoon oregano
2 cloves garlic, minced	¾ cup olive oil

Buy large, even-sized mushrooms. Wash but do not peel them. Remove the stems and chop; mix with the cheese, bread crumbs, onions, garlic, parsley, salt, pepper, and oregano. Stuff the mushroom cups.

Pour a little oil into a baking pan. Arrange the mushrooms in it. Pour the remaining oil over them, being sure to get a little on each mushroom. Bake in a 350° oven 25 minutes. Serve as an hors d'oeuvre, appetizer, or vegetable.

Serves 6-8

SPIEDINI alla ROMANA

Cheese and Anchovy Appetizer

1 loaf unsliced white bread	1 clove garlic, minced
1 pound mozzarella cheese	3 tablespoons wine vinegar
½ cup melted butter	¼ teaspoon freshly ground black pepper
3 tablespoons olive oil	
½ cup chopped anchovies	2 tablespoons minced parsley

Cut the bread into slices about ⅜ inch thick. Trim the crusts. Cut the slices into 1½-inch squares. Cut the cheese the same size. Thread the bread and cheese on six skewers, starting and ending with the bread. (Use about 6 pieces of bread and 4 of cheese for each skewer.) Arrange the skewers on a buttered baking pan; brush all sides with melted butter. Bake in a preheated 400° oven 10 minutes or until browned. Turn skewers to brown all sides. Slide off the skewers at the table. Prepare the sauce while the skewers are baking.

Heat the oil; stir in the anchovies and garlic until anchovies dissolve. Add the vinegar, pepper, and parsley; heat and serve in a sauceboat.

Serves 6.

MOZZARELLA alla MILANESE

Fried Cheese Sticks

1 pound Mozzarella cheese	2 eggs, beaten
½ cup flour	½ cup dry bread crumbs
1½ cups vegetable oil	

Slice the cheese ¼ inch thick, then into sticks 4 inches long by ½ inch wide. Roll in the flour, then dip in the eggs and finally in the bread crumbs, coating them well.

Heat the oil in a skillet until it bubbles. Fry a few sticks at a time until browned. Drain and serve hot.

Makes about 16 sticks.

Chapter 3

Soup

STRACIATELLA alla ROMANA

Egg-Ribbon Soup

3 eggs	2 tablespoons minced parsley
1 tablespoon cold water	6 cups chicken broth
¼ cup grated Romano or Parmesan cheese	

Beat the eggs and water in a bowl; stir in the cheese and parsley. Just before serving, bring the broth to a boil. Slowly pour the egg mixture into the soup, stirring steadily with a fork until eggs set. Serve immediately.

Serves 6-8.

ZUPPA alla PAVESE

Beef Soup with Eggs

4 cups chicken or beef broth	4 slices sautéed Italian or French bread, quartered
4 eggs	
Grated Parmesan cheese	

In a deep skillet bring the broth to a boil. Break 1 egg at a time into a saucer, then slide it gently into the broth. Cook until set, then skim out and place in a hot soup plate. Bring the broth to a boil again, then strain over the eggs. Arrange the bread around the eggs and sprinkle with cheese.

Serves 4.

PASTA in BRODO con FEGATINI

Noodle Soup, Milan Style

½ pound chicken livers	1 cup cooked fine noodles
3 tablespoons butter	1 cup firmly cooked green
½ teaspoon salt	peas
5 cups chicken broth	Grated Parmesan cheese

Wash the livers, cutting away any discolored spots. Chop the livers coarsely, then sauté in the butter 3 minutes; season with the salt.

Bring the broth to a boil; add the livers, noodles, and green peas. Cook over low heat 2 minutes. Taste for seasoning and serve with the grated cheese.

Serves 5-6.

ZUPPA alla VENEZIANA

Puréed Vegetable Soup

1½ cups dried white beans	1½ teaspoons salt
¼ cup olive oil	½ teaspoon freshly ground
1 cup chopped onions	black pepper
1 cup chopped carrots	½ teaspoon oregano
1 cup sliced celery	1 cup peeled diced tomatoes
1 cup diced potatoes	1 cup cooked vermicelli or
2 quarts beef broth	fine noodles
Grated Parmesan cheese	

Wash the beans, cover with water and bring to a boil. Cook 5 minutes, remove from the heat and let soak 1 hour. Drain.

Heat the oil in a saucepan; sauté the onions, carrots, celery, and potatoes 15 minutes. Add the beans and broth; bring to a boil and cook over low heat 1½ hours. Purée the vegetables in an electric blender of force through a sieve. Return to the saucepan; add the salt, pepper, and oregano. Cook 10 minutes. (If too thick, add a little broth or water.) Mix in the tomatoes; cook 1 minute, then add the vermicelli. Serve with grated Parmesan cheese.

Serves 6-8.

MINESTRONE alla MILANESE

Vegetable Soup, Milan Style

1 cup dried white beans	1 cup peeled diced tomatoes
2½ quarts water	3 cups shredded cabbage
3 slices bacon, diced	1 tablespoon salt
2 tablespoons olive oil	½ teaspoon freshly ground
1 cup thinly sliced onions	black pepper
1 carrot, diced	1 clove garlic, minced
1 cup diced potatoes	½ teaspoon basil
2 cups diced zucchini	¼ cup raw rice

½ cup grated Parmesan cheese

Wash the beans, cover with water, and bring to a boil. Let soak 1 hour, drain, and add the 2½ quarts water. Bring to a boil and cook over low heat 1½ hours. Meanwhile, prepare the vegetables.

In a skillet, lightly brown the bacon. Pour off the fat. Add the oil and onions. Sauté 5 minutes. Mix in the carrot, potatoes, and zucchini; sauté 5 minutes, stirring frequently. Add to the beans (after they have cooked 1½ hours) with the tomatoes, cabbage, salt, pepper, garlic, and basil. Cook over low heat 1¼ hours. Mix in the rice

Serves 8-10.

and parsley; cook 20 minutes longer. Just before serving, stir in the cheese. Serve with additional grated cheese.

MINESTRONE alla GENOVESE

Vegetable Soup, Genoa style

- 2 cups dried white beans
- 4 dried mushrooms
- 6 tablespoons olive oil
- ½ cup chopped onions
- 4 cups diced eggplant
- 4 cups shredded cabbage
- 2 cups sliced zucchini
- 2 cups peeled diced tomatoes or 2 cups canned
- 2½ quarts boiling water
- ½ cup vermicelli
- 2 teaspoons salt
- ½ teaspoon freshly grated black pepper
- ½ cup minced parsley
- ½ teaspoon basil
- 2 cloves garlic, minced
- ⅓ cup pine nuts or sliced blanched almonds
- ⅓ cup grated Parmesan cheese

Wash the beans, cover them with water and bring to a boil, let soak 1 hour. Drain. Cover with fresh water, bring to a boil, and cook 1½ hours. Drain. Wash the mushrooms, cover with warm water, and let soak 10 minutes. Drain and slice.

Heat 3 tablespoons oil in a saucepan; sauté the onions 5 minutes. Stir in eggplant, cabbage, and zucchini until coated with the oil. Add tomatoes, water, and beans. Bring to a boil and cook over low heat 30 minutes. Mix in the vermicelli, salt, and pepper; cook 10 minutes or until vermicelli is tender.

In an electric blender combine parsley, basil, garlic, nuts, cheese, and remaining oil. Turn motor on until paste is formed. Or pound ingredients to a paste, gradually adding the oil. Stir into the soup.

Serves 8-10.

ZUPPA di FAGIOLI e RISO

Beans and Rice Soup

1 cup dried white beans	1½ cups peeled chopped tomatoes
7 cups water	2 teaspoons salt
3 tablespoons olive oil	⅛ teaspoon crushed dried
1 cup chopped onions	red pepper
1 stalk celery, diced	½ cup raw rice
1 clove garlic, minced	2 tablespoons minced parsley
Grated Romano or Parmesan cheese	

Wash the beans, cover with water, and bring to a boil. Let soak 1 hour. Drain, add 7 cups water, bring to a boil, and cook over low heat 2 hours or until the beans are tender.

Heat the oil in a skillet; sauté the onions, celery, and garlic 5 minutes. Add the tomatoes, salt, and red peppers; cook over low heat 5 minutes. Add to the beans with the rice. Cook 25 minutes. Stir in the parsley and taste for seasoning. Serve with the cheese. This is a very thick soup—you may thin it with a little broth if you like.

Serves 6-8.

ZUPPA di FAGIOLI alla TOSCANA

Bean Soup, Tuscan Style

2 cups dried white beans	¼ cup olive oil
2 quarts water	¼ cup finely chopped onions
1 bay leaf	2 cloves garlic, minced
2 teaspoons salt	3 tablespoons minced parsley
½ teaspoon freshly ground black pepper	

Wash the beans, cover with water, and bring to a boil. Let soak 1 hour. Drain. Add the 2 quarts water and the bay leaf. Bring to a boil and cook over low heat 2½ hours. Purée half the beans in an electric blender or force through a sieve. Return to the balance of the soup; mix in the salt and pepper.

Heat the oil in a skillet; sauté the onions 10 minutes. Mix in the garlic; sauté 1 minute. Add to the soup with the parsley. Cook 10 minutes. Taste for seasoning.

Serves 6-8.

MINESTRINA di RISO

Rice Soup

7 cups chicken or beef broth	2 tablespoons cold water
1 cup raw washed rice	¼ cup grated Parmesan cheese
2 egg yolks	
2 tablespoons lemon juice	

Bring the broth to a boil; stir in the rice. Cook over medium heat 20 minutes.

Beat the egg yolks in a tureen or bowl. Beat in the lemon juice, water, and cheese. Gradually add the soup, stirring constantly.

Serves 6-7.

ZUPPA di ASPARAGI

Cream of Asparagus Soup

2 pounds asparagus or 2 packages frozen, thawed	2 quarts water
3 cups sliced potatoes	2 teaspoons salt
1 cup sliced leeks	¼ teaspoon white pepper
½ cup sliced onions	2 tablespoons butter
	1 egg yolk
1 cup heavy cream	

Wash the fresh asparagus, cut away the tough white part and discard. Cut off twelve 1½-inch pieces from the tip end and reserve. Or cut off twelve 1½-inch tips from the frozen asparagus and reserve. Slice the remaining fresh or frozen asparagus in 1-inch pieces. Combine in a saucepan with the potatoes, leeks, onions, water, salt, and pepper. Bring to a boil and cook over low heat 35 minutes. Purée in an electric blender, then strain, or force through a sieve.

Return to the saucepan and add the reserved tips and butter. Cook over low heat 10 minutes.

Beat the egg yolk and cream in a bowl; add a little of the hot soup, stirring steadily to prevent curdling. Return to balance of the soup. Heat, but do not let boil. Serve with a couple of asparagus tips in each plate, and with croutons.

Serves 6-8.

ZUPPA di CASTAGNE

Chestnut Soup

¾ pound chestnuts
2 tablespoons butter
1 cup chopped onions
½ cup sliced carrots
1½ quarts chicken broth
1½ teaspoons salt
¼ teaspoon white pepper
1 cup light cream

Cut a crisscross on the pointed end of the chestnuts. Cover with water, bring to a boil, and cook over low heat 15 minutes. Drain, peel, and remove the inner skins.

Melt the butter in a saucepan; sauté the onions and carrots 10 minutes. Add the broth, salt, pepper, and chestnuts. Bring to a boil and cook over low heat 30 minutes or until chestnuts are very tender. Purée in an electric blender or force through a sieve. Return to the saucepan; stir in the cream. Heat and taste for seasoning.

Serves 6-8.

PAPAROT

Spinach-Corn Meal Soup

1 pound spinach, or
  1 package frozen
3 tablespoons butter
1 clove garlic, minced
1 tablespoon flour
2 teaspoons salt
¼ teaspoon freshly ground
  black pepper
⅛ teaspoon nutmeg
1½ quarts water
3 tablespoons yellow corn meal

Cook the spinach 3 minutes; drain well, then chop coarsely.

Melt the butter in a saucepan; sauté the garlic 1 minute. Blend in the flour, salt, pepper, and nutmeg, then the spinach. Cover and cook over low heat 2 minutes. Add the water, bring to a boil, and cook over low heat 5 minutes. Stir in the corn meal; cook 20 minutes, stirring frequently. Taste for seasoning.

Serves 6-8.

ZUPPA di SPINACI

Spinach-Egg Soup

2 pounds spinach or
  2 packages frozen
4 tablespoons butter
1¼ teaspoons salt
½ teaspoon white pepper
⅛ teaspoon nutmeg
4 egg yolks
¼ cup grated Parmesan
  cheese
6 cups boiling chicken broth

Cook the spinach 4 minutes. Drain thoroughly. Purée in an electric blender or force through a sieve.

Melt the butter in a saucepan; add the spinach, salt, pepper, and nutmeg. Cook over low heat 2 minutes, stirring almost constantly. Beat the egg yolks and cheese; mix into the spinach. Gradually add the broth, stirring constantly. Bring to a boil (the eggs will curdle, so don't worry) and serve with croutons.

Serves 8.

ZUPPA di POMIDORO

Cream of Tomato Soup

4 tablespoons butter	¼ teaspoon freshly ground black pepper
1¼ cups chopped onions	1 teaspoon sugar
2 pounds tomatoes, peeled and diced	2 cups hot chicken broth
1 teaspoon salt	1 cup sour cream

Melt the butter in a saucepan; sauté the onions 10 minutes. Add the tomatoes, salt, pepper, and sugar. Bring to a boil and cook over low heat 20 minutes. Purée in an electric blender or force through a sieve. Blend in the broth and sour cream. Return to saucepan, taste for seasoning, and heat but do not let boil.

Serves 4-6.

MINESTRA di LENTICCHIE

Lentil Soup

2 cups lentils	2 teaspoons salt
2½ quarts water	½ teaspoon freshly ground black pepper
¼ pound salt pork, diced	¼ teaspoon thyme
1 cup chopped onions	1 tablespoon butter
¼ cup grated carrots	

Wash the lentils thoroughly. Add the water; bring to a boil and cook over low heat 1 hour.

Brown the salt pork in a skillet. Remove the browned bits and reserve. Pour off all but 2 tablespoons fat. Sauté the onions and carrots in the fat for 10 minutes. Add to the lentils with salt, pepper, and thyme; cook 1 hour longer, or until lentils are tender. Purée in an electric blender or force through a sieve.

Return to the saucepan, stir in the butter and pork bits. Heat, taste for seasoning, and serve with sautéed Italian or French bread.

Serves 8-10.

ZUPPA di VERDURE

Potato-Vegetable Soup

4 tablespoons butter	6 cups boiling water
½ cup chopped onions	1 cup canned tomato sauce
½ cup sliced celery	3 cups diced potatoes
¾ cup sliced carrots	2 teaspoons salt
2 tablespoons minced parsley	½ teaspoon freshly ground
1 clove garlic, minced	black pepper
Grated Parmesan cheese	

Melt the butter in a saucepan; sauté the onions, celery, carrots, parsley, and garlic 10 minutes. Add the water, tomato sauce, potatoes, salt, and pepper. Bring to a boil and cook over low heat 30 minutes. Purée in an electric blender or force through sieve. Taste for seasoning; heat and serve with the cheese.

Serves 6-7.

ZUPPA di PESCE alla VENEZIANA

Fish Soup

3 pounds sliced assorted fish	½ teaspoon marjoram
2 fish heads and trimmings of fish	½ cup olive oil
	½ cup finely chopped onions
4 cups water	2 cloves garlic, minced
2½ teaspoons salt	1 cup dry white wine
½ teaspoon freshly ground black pepper	1 cup canned Italian-style tomatoes
1 cup sliced onions	¼ teaspoon saffron
1 bay leaf	2 tablespoons minced parsley

Buy at least 2 or 3 varieties of fish—red snapper, sea bass, pike, or whitefish are good. Have the fish cut in slices 1-inch thick, and then in half through the bone. Wash and dry the fish.

In a saucepan, combine the heads, trimmings, water,

salt, pepper, sliced onions, bay leaf, and marjoram. Bring to a boil and cook over low heat 45 minutes. Strain.

Heat the oil in a deep large skillet; sauté the chopped onions and garlic 5 minutes. Add the fish; brown on both sides. Add the wine; cook over medium heat 5 minutes. Add the tomatoes, saffron, parsley, and stock. Cook over low heat 15 minutes. Taste for seasoning. Serve in deep plates, with sauteéd sliced Italian or French bread.

Serves 6-8.

Chapter 4

Fish

SOGLIOLE alla VENEZIANA

Sole, Venetian Style

4 fillets of sole	6 tablespoons butter
½ cup flour	1 cup thinly sliced onions
1 clove garlic, minced	½ cup dry white wine
8 tablespoons minced parsley	½ cup water
2½ teaspoons salt	⅛ teaspoon rosemary
¾ teaspoon freshly ground black pepper	

Wash and dry the sole; dip in a mixture of the flour, garlic, parsley, 2 teaspoons salt, and ½ teaspoon pepper.

Melt 2 tablespoons butter in a saucepan; sauté the onions over very low heat 10 minutes. Add the wine, water, the remaining salt and pepper and the rosemary. Bring to a boil and cook over low heat 20 minutes, while preparing the fish.

Melt the remaining butter in a skillet; sauté the fillets until browned on both sides and fish flakes easily when tested with a fork. Transfer to a heated serving dish and pour the sauce over it.

Serves 4.

SOGLIOLE alla PARMIGIANA

Fillet of Sole with Parmesan cheese

4 fillets of sole	6 tablespoons butter
2 teaspoons salt	½ cup grated Parmesan cheese
½ teaspoon freshly ground black pepper	¼ cup bottled clam juice

Wash and dry the fillets. Season with the salt and pepper. Melt 4 tablespoons butter in a skillet; sauté the fish until browned on both sides. Sprinkle with the cheese. Dot with the remaining butter and add the clam juice. Cover and cook over low heat 5 minutes.

Serves 4.

SOGLIOLA MARINARA

Fillet of Sole, Fisherman's Style

4 fillets of sole	3 tablespoons butter
¼ cup flour	1 tablespoon olive oil
2 teaspoons salt	1 clove garlic, minced
½ teaspoon freshly ground black pepper	⅓ cup dry white wine
	2 tablespoons minced parsley

Wash and dry the fillets. Dip in a mixture of the flour, salt, and pepper.

Heat the butter and oil in a skillet; sauté the fillets 6 minutes, or until bottom is browned. Turn fillets over, add the garlic and sauté 5 minutes. Add the wine and parsley; cook over high heat 1 minute. Transfer the fillets to a heated serving dish; scrape the bottom of the skillet and pour over the fish.

Serves 4.

PESCE alla ROMANA

Fish with Mushroom-Wine Sauce

3 pound whole fish or 1 piece	6 anchovy fillets, chopped
2 teaspoons salt	2 cups dry white wine
½ teaspoon freshly ground black pepper	½ cup water
4 tablespoons butter	2 tablespoons olive oil
¾ cup chopped onions	½ pound mushrooms, sliced
1 clove garlic, minced	1 tablespoon flour
	2 tablespoons minced parsley

Buy sea bass, pike, or similar fish. If you can't get a whole fish, buy a piece of a large fish. Wash and dry the fish; rub with salt and pepper.

In a deep large skillet, melt the butter; sauté the onions 5 minutes. Mix in the garlic and anchovies for 1 minute. Add the wine and water. Bring to a boil and cook over low heat 5 minutes. Place the fish in the skillet. Cover loosely and cook over low heat 40 minutes or until fish flakes easily when tested with a fork. Carefully transfer fish to a heated serving dish and keep warm.

While the fish is cooking, prepare the mushrooms. Heat the oil in a saucepan; sauté the mushrooms 5 minutes. Sprinkle with the flour. Add the fish stock, stirring steadily to the boiling point. Mix in the parsley, cook over low heat 5 minutes. Pour over the fish.

Serves 4-6.

CACCIUCCO alla FIORENTINA

Fish Stew

4 pounds assorted fish (bass, whiting, snapper, eel)
1 lobster, cut up in the shell
Fish head and bones
¾ cup olive oil
3 cloves garlic, minced
3 sprigs parsley
½ cup celery leaves
½ teaspoon marjoram
1 tablespoon salt
½ teaspoon crushed dried red peppers
1 cup dry wine
½ cup dry white wine
2 cups water
2 tablespoons tomato paste
¼ cup diced celery
2 cloves garlic, sliced
3 tablespoons minced parsley
¼ teaspoon thyme

Wash and dry the fish and lobster. Almost any combination can be used, but be sure to have a lobster. The fish head and bones should be used, but if you can't get them, substitute 2 cups bottled clam juice for the water.

Heat ½ cup oil in a saucepan; sauté the garlic, sprigs of parsley and celery leaves 5 minutes. Add fish heads, marjoram, salt, red peppers, the wines, water, and tomato paste. Bring to a boil and cook over low heat 45 minutes. Strain, pressing through as much solids as possible.

Heat remaining oil in the saucepan; sauté diced celery, sliced garlic, minced parsley, and thyme 5 minutes. Arrange the fish over it and add the strained stock. Bring to a boil, cover and cook over low heat 10 minutes. Add the lobster, recover and cook 20 minutes longer. Taste for seasoning. Serve in deep bowls with toasted garlic bread.

Serves 6-8.

ARAGOSTA alla GRIGLIA

Broiled Lobster

1½ quarts water
1 cup dry white wine
1 onion
2 stalks celery
1 tablespoon salt
¼ teaspoon white pepper
1 bay leaf
4 live lobsters or 8 frozen lobster tails
¼ cup melted butter

Combine and bring to a boil the water, wine, onion, celery, salt, pepper, and bay leaf. Cook over medium heat 10 minutes. Plunge the lobsters into the liquid; cook 15 minutes. Drain, cool and split lobsters in half. Remove the vein and sacks.

Place on a baking pan; brush with butter. Broil 10 minutes. Serve with additional melted butter and lemon quarters.

Serves 4-8.

ARAGOSTA ALL'AMBASCIATORI

Lobster in Liquor Sauce

2 1½-pound lobsters or 4 lobster tails	¼ cup cognac
⅓ cup butter	¼ cup gin
⅓ cup olive oil	½ cup dry white wine
⅓ cup minced shallots or sweet onions	2 cups heavy cream
	2 teaspoons salt
1 clove garlic, minced	½ teaspoon white pepper
	1 tablespoon lemon juice

Cut the lobster into sections in the shell. If there is any coral in the live lobsters, set it aside.

Heat the butter and oil in a deep skillet; cook the lobsters over high heat until red. Pour off the fat; add the shallots, garlic, cognac, and gin; cook until the liquid is evaporated. Add the wine; again let evaporate. Add the cream, salt, and pepper; cover and cook over low heat 20 minutes. Remove the meat from the lobster shells and keep warm. If there is any coral reserved, mix it into the sauce with the lemon juice; if not, just add the lemon juice. Reduce to 1 cup. Strain and pour over the lobster.

Serves 2-4.

COZZE alla MARINARA

Mussels in Wine

60 mussels	3 cloves garlic, minced
⅓ cup olive oil	½ teaspoon freshly ground black pepper
1½ cups dry white wine	
½ cup minced parsley	

Scrub the mussels and remove the beards. Wash under cold running water for several minutes.

Heat the oil and wine in a kettle; mix in the garlic and

pepper. Add the mussels. Cover loosely and cook over high heat 5 minutes or until open. Remove the mussels to deep dishes; stir the parsley into the broth. Pour over the mussels.

Serves 4-6.

SCAMPI alla LAGO di COMO

Shrimp, Lake Como Style

3 tablespoons olive oil	1 cup peeled chopped tomatoes
3 tablespoons butter	1 teaspoon salt
¼ cup minced onion	¼ teaspoon freshly ground black pepper
2 tablespoons grated carrot	
1 bay leaf, finely chopped	1 tablespoon lemon juice
1½ pounds raw shrimp, shelled and deveined	¾ cup bottle clam juice
⅓ cup warm cognac	1 teaspoon flour
	¾ cup heavy cream

Heat the oil and 2 tablespoons butter in a skillet; sauté the onion, carrot, and bay leaf 10 minutes. Add the shrimp; sauté 3 minutes. Pour the warm brandy over the shrimp and set it aflame. When flames die, add the tomatoes, salt, pepper, lemon juice, and clam juice. Cook over low heat 8 minutes.

Remove the shrimp to a warm serving dish. Cook the sauce over high heat 2 minutes. Cream the flour with the remaining butter and add to the sauce with the cream. Cook over low heat 3 minutes, stirring steadily. Pour over the shrimp.

Serves 4-6.

SCAMPI alla MARINARA

Shrimp, Fisherman's Style

Sauce:

4 tablespoons olive oil	1½ teaspoons salt
¾ cup finely chopped onions	½ teaspoon freshly ground
½ cup grated carrots	black pepper
2 pounds tomatoes, chopped	½ teaspoon basil
1 clove garlic, minced	

Heat the oil in a saucepan; sauté the onions 10 minutes. Mix in the carrots; sauté 2 minutes. Add the tomatoes, garlic, salt, pepper, and basil; cook over low heat 45 minutes, stirring frequently. Purée in an electric blender or force through sieve. Return to the saucepan.

Shrimp:

3 tablespoons butter	1¼ teaspoons salt
2 pounds raw shrimp, shelled and deveined	¼ teaspoon freshly ground black pepper
1 clove garlic, minced	¼ cup chopped parsley

Melt the butter in a skillet. Add the shrimp, garlic, salt, and pepper. Sauté 3 minutes, shaking the pan frequently. Add to the sauce with the parsley; cook over low heat 10 minutes.

Serves 6-8.

SCAMPI alla SPIEDO

Shrimp on Skewers

24 raw shrimp, shelled and deveined	1 bay leaf crushed to a powder
1½ teaspoons salt	½ teaspoon thyme
½ teaspoon freshly ground black pepper	¼ cup olive oil

Wash and dry the shrimp. Toss with a mixture of the salt, pepper, bay leaf, and thyme. Thread on 4 skewers; brush with the oil. Broil 12 minutes; turning the skewers frequently and brush with oil each time. Serve with lemon wedges.

Serves 4.

GAMBERITTI in CREMA

Shrimp in Cream

6 tablespoons butter
¾ cup minced onions
¼ cup minced celery
½ cup grated carrots
¼ teaspoon marjoram
2 pounds raw shrimp, shelled and deveined
3 tablespoons warm cognac
3 tablespoons flour
2 cups light cream
3 tablespoons sweet vermouth
1¼ teaspoons salt

Melt the butter in a skillet; sauté the onions, celery, carrots, and marjoram 10 minutes. Add the shrimp, sauté 5 minutes, stirring frequently. Pour the cognac over the shrimp and set aflame. When flames die, remove the shrimp. Blend the flour into the skillet, then add the cream, stirring steadily to the boiling point. Cook over low heat 5 minutes. Mix in the vermouth and salt and return the shrimp. Cook over low heat 5 minutes. Serve with rice. The sauce may be strained if you like.

Serves 6-8.

RISOTTO di SCAMPI

Shrimp Risotto

6 tablespoons butter	1 pound cooked, cleaned
3 tablespoons olive oil	shrimp
1 clove garlic, minced	1½ teaspoons salt
1½ cups raw rice	¼ teaspoon white pepper
¾ cup dry white wine	¼ teaspoon marjoram
4 cups hot chicken broth	3 tablespoons grated
3 tablespoons grated Parmesan Cheese	

Heat 4 tablespoons butter and the oil in a heavy skillet or casserole. Stir in the garlic and rice until golden. Add the wine; cook over medium heat until absorbed. Add half the broth; cover and cook over low heat 15 minutes. Add the shrimp, salt, pepper, marjoram, and remaining broth. Stir lightly with a fork. Recover and cook 10 minutes over low heat or until rice is tender and dry. Stir in the cheese and remaining butter.

Serves 4-6.

FRITTELE di ARAGOSTA o SCAMPI

Fried Lobster or Shrimp

1 cup sifted flour	3 live lobsters or 1½ pounds
1⅛ teaspoons salt	shrimp
¾ cup lukewarm water	¼ teaspoon freshly ground
3 tablespoons olive or	black pepper
vegetable oil	1 egg white
Vegetable oil for deep frying	

Sift the flour and ⅛ teaspoon salt into a bowl. Stir in the water, then the oil until very smooth. Set aside for 2 hours.

Cut the meat of the lobster into bite-sized pieces. Or shell and devein the shrimp. Or use a mixture of both. Season with the pepper and remaining salt.

Beat the egg white until stiff but not dry; fold it into the batter. Dip the seafood into it. Heat the oil to 360° and fry the seafood until browned. Drain well. Serve with mayonnaise.

Serves 4-6 as a first course.

SCAMPI FRITTI

Fried Shrimp

1½ pounds raw shrimp, shelled and deveined	½ teaspoon freshly ground black pepper
⅓ cup flour	1 cup olive or vegetable oil
1½ teaspoons salt	Lemon wedges

Wash and dry the shrimp; toss in a mixture of the flour, salt, and pepper. Heat the oil in a skillet; fry the shrimp until browned on both sides. Drain. Serve with the lemon wedges.

Serves 4-6.

Chapter 5

Eggs and Cheese

FRITTATA al FORMAGGIO

Cheese Omelet

3 eggs	4 tablespoons grated Parmesan cheese
1 tablespoon water	1 tablespoon minced parsley
¼ teaspoon salt	2 tablespoons butter
⅛ teaspoon white pepper	

Beat the eggs, water, salt, and pepper until slightly frothy. Stir in the cheese and parsley.

Melt the butter in a 9-inch skillet until it bubbles. Pour in the egg mixture; cook over medium heat until bottom browns lightly. Lift the edges to allow the unset part to run under, then turn over to brown other side. (Put a plate over the pan, and turn omelet onto it, then slide it back into the pan.) Turn out flat onto a heated serving dish.

Serves 2.

FRITTATA di SPINACI

Spinach Pancake Omelet

3 tablespoons olive oil	⅛ teaspoon thyme
¼ cup minced onions	¼ cup grated Parmesan cheese
1 clove garlic	
4 eggs	1 cup chopped cooked spinach
1 teaspoon salt	½ cup dry bread crumbs
⅛ teaspoon freshly ground black pepper	

Heat 1 tablespoon oil in a skillet; sauté the onions and garlic until soft and yellow. Discard the garlic. Beat together the eggs, salt, pepper, and thyme. Mix in the cheese, spinach, bread crumbs, onions and 1 tablespoon oil. Taste for seasoning.

Wipe the skillet clean of any onions. Heat the remaining oil in the skillet; pour the mixture into it. Cook over low heat until shrunk away from the sides of the pan, then place under a hot broiler to brown the top.

Serves 3-4.

FRITTATA

Vegetable Omelet

3 tablespoons olive oil	2 teaspoons salt
½ cup chopped onions	½ teaspoon freshly ground black pepper
½ cup sliced mushrooms	6 eggs
½ cup sliced zucchini	½ cup canned tomato sauce
½ package frozen artichoke hearts, thawed	

Heat the oil in a skillet (with ovenproof handle); sauté the onions 5 minutes. Add the mushrooms, zucchini, and artichokes; sauté 10 minutes. Season with half the salt and pepper.

Beat the eggs with the remaining salt and pepper; pour over the vegetables. Spoon the tomato sauce over the top. Bake in a preheated 350° oven 15 minutes or until set. Serve at once, cut in wedges. The *Frittata* may also be baked in individual dishes, in which case serve in the dish.

Serves 4-6.

TORTINO d'UOVA

Baked Eggs in Potato Nests

2 cups seasoned mashed potatoes	¼ teaspoon freshly ground black pepper
8 thin slices mozzarella cheese	4 tablespoons grated Parmesan cheese
4 eggs	2 tablespoons butter
1 teaspoon salt	

Spread 4 individual buttered baking dishes with the potatoes. Cover with 2 slices of cheese. Make an indentation in each dish and carefully break an egg into it. Sprinkle with the salt, pepper and grated cheese; dot with the butter.

Bake in a preheated 425° oven 8 minutes or until eggs are set and cheese melted.

Serves 4.

UOVA FIORENTINA

Eggs and Spinach

2 pounds spinach or 2 packages frozen, thawed	⅛ teaspoon white pepper
4 tablespoons olive oil	8 eggs
¾ teaspoon salt	4 tablespoons grated Parmesan cheese

Wash the fresh spinach and drain well. Or drain the frozen spinach. Heat the oil in a skillet. Add the fresh or frozen spinach, the salt and pepper. Cook over low heat 5 minutes, stirring frequently. Drain and chop fine.

Divide the spinach among 4 individual buttered serving dishes. Make 2 indentations in each and carefully break an egg into each. Sprinkle with the cheese. Bake in a preheated 350° oven 8 minutes, or until set.

Serves 4.

UOVA alla CACCIATORA

Eggs, Hunter's Style

- ¼ pound chicken livers
- 4 tablespoons olive oil
- ¼ cup chopped onions
- 1¼ teaspoons salt
- ¼ teaspoon freshly ground black pepper
- ¼ teaspoon basil
- ¼ cup canned tomato sauce
- ¼ cup dry white wine
- 4 eggs
- 4 slices buttered toast
- 1 tablespoon parsley

Wash the livers, removing any discolored areas. Cut each half in 2 pieces.

Heat the oil in a skillet; sauté the onions 5 minutes. Add the livers; sauté 5 minutes, mixing a few times. Add the salt, pepper, basil, tomato sauce, and wine. Bring to a boil and cook over low heat 5 minutes. Carefully break the eggs into the pan, cover and cook until set, about 3 minutes. Carefully put an egg on each piece of toast and cover with the sauce. Sprinkle with the parsley.

Serves 2-4.

UOVA alla PARMIGIANA

Eggs, Parma Style

- ¼ pound prosciutto or cooked ham, cut julienne
- 8 eggs
- 1 teaspoon salt
- ¼ teaspoon white pepper
- ½ cup grated Parmesan cheese
- 4 tablespoons melted butter

Lightly brown the ham and drain. Use 4 buttered individual shallow, baking dishes, and into each carefully put 2 eggs. Season with salt and pepper and put the ham over them. Sprinkle with the cheese and butter. Bake in a 350° oven 10 minutes or until the eggs are set. Serve in the dishes.

Serves 4.

FRITTATINE IMBOCCICE

Stuffed Pancakes

Pancakes:

1 cup sifted flour
½ teaspoon salt
1 egg
½ cup milk
½ cup water
2 tablespoons vegetable oil
2 tablespoons butter

Sift the flour and salt into a bowl; beat in the egg, milk and water until smooth, then stir in the oil. Chill 2 hours. Beat again—the mixture should be like cream —if too thick, add a little more milk.

Melt a little butter in a 7-inch skillet; when it bubbles, pour in just enough butter to thinly coat the bottom, about 1 tablespoon. Cook just until set and lightly browned, then turn over. Stack while preparing the balance.

Filling:

½ cup grated Swiss cheese
1 cup grated Parmesan cheese
1 egg, beaten
¼ cup milk
¼ teaspoon white pepper
¼ teaspoon nutmeg
3 tablespoons butter
½ cup chicken broth

Mix together the Swiss cheese, ½ cup Parmesan cheese, the egg, milk, pepper, and nutmeg. Place a heaping tablespoon on each pancake and roll up. Arrange in a single layer, in a buttered shallow baking dish. Dot with the butter, sprinkle with the remaining cheese and add the broth. Bake in a preheated 350° oven 15 minutes or until browned.

Makes about 12.

FONDUTA

Cheese-Truffle Fondue

1 pound Fontina cheese or
   ¾ pound mozzarella and
   ¼ pound Bel Paese
1 tablespoon corn starch
1 cup milk
3 tablespoons butter
½ teaspoon salt
¼ teaspoon white pepper
4 egg yolks, beaten
White truffles, sliced
Sautéed sliced Italian or
   French bread

Fontina cheese is customarily used in Fonduta, but it isn't readily available in the United States. The combination of cheeses makes a good substitute. Dice the cheese.

Mix the corn starch with the milk; combine in the top of a chafing dish or double boiler with the cheese, butter, salt, and pepper. Place over hot water and cook, stirring steadily, until cheese melts. Very gradually beat in the egg yolks, stirring constantly until thickened. Do not let boil. Serve in the chafing dish, or if prepared in the double boiler, pour into a hot serving dish. Sprinkle with the truffles and surround with the bread.

Serves 4-6.

Chapter 6

Pastas and Sauces

PASTA al UOVO
Egg Dough (for Cannelloni, Lasagne, Fettucini)

4 cups sifted flour	3 whole eggs, beaten
1 teaspoon salt	2 egg yolks, beaten

Sift the flour and salt into a bowl. Make a well in the center and into it put the eggs and egg yolks. Work in the flour with the fingers. Turn out onto a floured surface and knead until smooth and elastic with floured hands. Form into a ball and cover with a bowl for 20 minutes. Divide the dough into 3 pieces. Roll out each piece paper thin—roll in one direction, sprinkling with flour from time to time.

Cannelonni:

Cut dough into 4-inch squares. Drop a few at a time into boiling salted water; cook 2 minutes, then remove with a slotted spoon and drop into cold salted water. Drain and dry on a towel. Fill as desired and proceed as directed for individual fillings.

Lasagne:

Sprinkle the rolled dough with flour. Cut into strips 2-inches wide and 6-inches long. Cook in boiling salted water 6 minutes (if not to be baked), 3 minutes (if to be baked).

Fettuccine:

Sprinkle the rolled dough with flour. Cut into long strips ½ inch wide. Spread on a cloth to dry for 1 hour before cooking. Cook in boiling salted water 6 minutes or until tender but still firm. Drain well. Use as directed in recipes. Uncooked fettuccine may be stored for future use.

CANNELLONI

Egg Pasta (see recipe)
1 cup cooked spinach
1 cup ricotta cheese
2 tablespoons melted butter
½ cup Tomato Sauce (see recipe)
½ cup grated Parmesan cheese

Prepare the egg pasta and roll into 2 paper-thin sheets, well sprinkled with flour. Cut into 3 by 4 inch rectangles, then let dry 1 hour. Cook in boiling salted water 5 minutes. Drain, rinse with cold water, and spread on a towel to dry.

Purée the spinach in a electric blender or chop very fine. Mix with the ricotta cheese, butter, and ¼ cup Parmesan cheese. Spread on the cooked dough and roll up like a jelly roll.

Spread half the tomato sauce on the bottom of a shallow baking dish. Arrange the cannelloni in it; cover with the remaining tomato sauce and sprinkle with the remaining Parmesan cheese. Bake in a 450° oven 10 minutes.

Serves 6.

CANNELLONI

Rich Cheese-Stuffed Noodles

3 cups sifted flour
¾ teaspoon salt
2 whole eggs
2 eggs yolks
3 cups grated mozzarella or Swiss cheese
¾ cup grated Parmesan cheese
3 tablespoons very soft butter
2 cups fresh tomato sauce (see recipe)
2 tablespoons butter

Sift the flour and salt into a bowl. Make a well in the center and into it put the whole eggs and egg yolks. Work in the flour until smooth. Knead on a lightly floured surface until very smooth and elastic. Cover with a bowl and let stand 20 minutes.

Divide the dough in 3 parts; roll out each part until almost transparent. Cut into 4-inch squares. Cook in boiling salted water (a few at a time) 1½ minutes. Drop each batch into cold water. Drain well.

Mix together the cheese and softened butter. Spread the squares with the cheese mixture and roll up. Arrange (in a single layer) in a buttered baking dish. Cover with the tomato sauce and dot with the 2 tablespoons butter. Bake in a 300° oven 20 minutes. Serve with additional grated Parmesan cheese.

Serves 6-8.

LASAGNE VERDI alla BOLOGNESE
Green Noodles

Noodles:

½ pound spinach
4 cups sifted flour
1½ teaspoons salt

3 eggs, beaten
4 tablespoons butter
½ cup grated Parmesan cheese

Wash and drain the spinach. Cook over low heat 5 minutes. Drain very well. Purée in an electric blender, or force through a sieve, or chop very fine. If spinach is wet, place over low heat until moisture evaporates.

Sift the flour and salt into a bowl. Make a well in the center and into it put the eggs and spinach. Work in the flour with the hands. Turn out onto a floured surface and knead until smooth and elastic. Form into a ball and cover with a bowl; let stand 20 minutes.

Divide dough into 4 pieces and roll out each piece paper-thin, sprinkling with flour as you roll. Let dry 1 hour, then cut into 4-inch squares. Cook a few at a time in boiling salted water 2 minutes. Remove with a slotted spoon and drop into cold salted water. Drain and place on a cloth to dry.

In a buttered baking dish, spread a little Bolognese sauce (see recipe). Make as many successive layers as possible of the noodles, sauce, and grated cheese. End with sauce and cheese. Dot with the butter. Bake in a 375° oven 25 minutes.

Serves 6-8.

SPAGHETTI al TARTUFATA

Spaghetti with Truffle Sauce

1 can anchovy fillets	1¾ cups water
¼ cup olive oil	¼ teaspoon freshly ground
4 tablespoons butter	black peppers
3 cloves garlic, split	1 pound spaghetti, cooked
3 tablespoons tomato paste	and drained
4 or more truffles, cut julienne	

Drain, wash, drain, and chop the anchovies. Heat the oil and butter in a saucepan; sauté the garlic 3 minutes, then remove. With a wooden spoon, mix in the anchovies. Stir in the tomato paste mixed with the water and the pepper. Bring to a boil, and cook over low heat 20 minutes. Add the truffles; taste for seasoning.

Have the drained spaghetti in a heated deep serving dish. Pour the sauce over it and toss together.

Serves 4-6.

SPAGHETTI all'AMATRICIANA

Spaghetti with Bacon Sauce

¼ pound bacon, diced	⅛ teaspoon dried crushed red
1 pound tomatoes, peeled and chopped	peppers
¾ cup dry white wine	1 pound spaghetti, cooked and drained
½ teaspoon salt	

In a saucepan, cook the bacon until lightly browned but not crisp. Pour off half the fat. Add the tomatoes, wine, salt and pepper; bring to a boil and cook over low heat 25 minutes. Taste for seasoning and pour over the spaghetti.

Serves 4.

SPAGHETTI alla CAMPAGNOLA

Thin Spaghetti with Mushrooms and Anchovies

¼ cup olive oil	1 pound tomatoes, peeled and chopped
6 anchovy fillets, minced	
2 cloves garlic, minced	1 pound spaghettini, cooked and drained
¼ pound mushrooms, sliced	
¾ cup dry white wine	3 tablespoons minced parsley
⅛ teaspoon diced crushed red peppers	

Heat the oil in a saucepan; sauté the anchovies and garlic 2 minutes. Add the mushrooms; cook 2 minutes. Mix in the wine; cook over high heat 2 minutes. Add the peppers and tomatoes. Cook over low heat 20 minutes. Taste for seasoning. Pour over the spaghettini and sprinkle with the parsley.

Serves 4.

FETTUCINE all'ALFREDO

Egg Noodles with Butter and Cheese

1 pound fettucine or broad egg noodles (home made, if possible)

¼ pound butter

1 cup freshly grated Parmesan cheese

Very thin noodles are best, but if you don't want to make them, buy fettucine or broad noodles. Cook them in boiling salted water until tender but still firm. Drain. Have ready a heated deep serving dish, with the butter broken into pieces in it. Put the fettucine on it and sprinkle with the cheese. Quickly and lightly, using a fork and spoon, toss the fettucine until well coated with butter and cheese.

Serves 4.

SPAGHETTI alla CARBONARA

Spaghetti with Ham Sauce

- 3 slices bacon, cut julienne
- 4 tablespoons olive oil
- 2 tablespoons butter
- ½ cup julienne-cut ham (prosciutto, if available)
- 4 tablespoons grated Parmesan cheese
- 2 eggs, beaten
- 1 pound spaghetti, cooked and drained

In a skillet, brown the bacon lightly; pour off the fat. Add the oil, butter, and ham. Sauté 5 minutes, but do not let the ingredients brown. Remove from the heat and stir in the cheese, then the eggs. Pour quickly over the hot spaghetti and mix thoroughly.

Serves 4-6.

SPAGHETTI alla VONGOLE (ROSSO)

Spaghetti with Red Clam Sauce

- ⅓ cup olive oil
- 1 cup chopped onions
- 3 cloves garlic, minced
- 3 cups chopped tomatoes
- 1½ teaspoons salt
- ½ teaspoon freshly ground black pepper
- 2 quarts small hard shell clams
- 1 pound spaghetti, cooked and drained
- ¼ cup finely chopped parsley

Heat the oil in a saucepan; sauté the onions 10 minutes. Add the garlic, tomatoes, salt, and pepper. Cook over low heat 45 minutes. Purée half the sauce in an electric blender or force through a sieve. Return to the saucepan. Taste for seasoning.

While the sauce is cooking, scrub the clams and wash under cold running water until water runs clean. Put in a pan; cover and cook over high heat until shells open; shake the pan frequently. Discard any clams that do not open. Strain the juice. Add to the tomato sauce with the clams and parsley. Heat. Spoon over the spaghetti. (No cheese is served with this dish).

Serves 4-6.

Note: The clams may be removed from the shells before combining with the tomato sauce.

SPAGHETTI alla VONGOLE (BIANCO)

Spaghetti with White Clam Sauce

2 quarts small hard shell clams	¼ teaspoon freshly ground black pepper
½ cup olive oil	
¾ cup finely chopped onions	1 pound spaghetti, cooked and drained
2 cloves garlic, minced	
⅓ cup minced parsley	

Scrub the clams; wash under cold running water until water runs clean. Put in a saucepan; cover and cook over high heat until shells open, shaking the pan frequently. Remove the clams and strain the juice. While the clams are being steamed, prepare the sauce.

Heat the oil in a saucepan; sauté the onions 5 minutes. Add the garlic, sauté 5 minutes. Add the steamed clams, juice, pepper, and parsley; cook 1 minute. Spoon over the spaghetti. (No cheese is served with this dish.)

Serves 4-6.

Note: The clams may be removed from the shells before combining with the sauce.

FETTUCCINE alla PAPALINA

Noodles with Egg Sauce

¼ pound butter	4 egg yolks
½ cup chopped onions	4 tablespoons freshly grated Parmesan cheese
¼ pound prosciutto or cooked ham, cut julienne	1 pound fettuccine (see recipe) or broad egg noodles, cooked and drained
½ cup sliced, sautéed mushrooms	

Melt 2 tablespoons butter in a skillet; sauté the onions and ham 5 minutes. Stir in the sautéed mushrooms; season to taste.

Beat the egg yolks in the top of a double boiler. Stir in the cheese and the remaining butter, broken into small pieces. Place over hot (not boiling) water and stir constantly with a wooden spoon until thickened.

Put the drained fettuccine in a hot bowl; pour the egg mixture over it and toss until well distributed. Sprinkle the ham mixture on the top.

Serves 4.

PAPPARDELLE alla TOSCANA

Broad Noodles with Tomato-Meat Sauce

5 dried mushrooms	1 cup dry red wine
4 tablespoons olive oil	1½ cups peeled chopped tomatoes
2 tablespoons butter	
½ cup chopped onions	1 teaspoon salt
¼ pound prosciutto or cooked ham, cut julienne	½ teaspoon freshly ground black pepper
¼ pound chicken livers, diced	1 pound broad noodles, cooked and drained
2 teaspoons flour	

This dish is best prepared with homemade noodles. Make egg dough recipe, and cut noodles 1½-inches wide or buy the broadest noodles available.

Wash the mushrooms, cover with warm water, and let soak 15 minutes. Drain and slice fine.

Heat the oil and butter in a saucepan; sauté the onions 5 minutes. Add the ham; sauté 5 minutes. Mix in the livers and mushrooms; sauté 3 minutes. Blend in the flour, then stir in the wine; cook over medium heat 5 minutes. Add the tomatoes, salt, and pepper; cook over low heat 25 minutes. Taste for seasoning.

Pour half the sauce over the noodles and toss. Serve with the remaining sauce.

Serves 4.

SOUFFLE di TAGLIARINI

Noodle Soufflé

- ¼ pound butter
- 3 tablespoons flour
- 1¼ teaspoons salt
- ¼ teaspoon white pepper
- 2 cups milk
- ½ cup heavy cream
- ½ cup grated Parmesan cheese
- 3 egg yolks, beaten
- ½ pound fine noodles, cooked and drained
- 5 egg whites, beaten stiff

Melt half the butter in a saucepan; blend in the flour, salt, and pepper. Add the milk and cream, stirring steadily to the boiling point. Cook over low heat 5 minutes. Mix in the cheese and remaining butter until melted. Remove from the heat.

Beat the egg yolks in a bowl; gradually add the sauce, stirring steadily to prevent curdling. Mix in the noodles, taste for seasoning. Cool 15 minutes, then fold in the egg whites.

Turn into a buttered 2-quart soufflé dish. Bake in a preheated 375° oven 25 minutes, or until browned and set.

Serves 4-6.

RAVIOLI

Egg Pasta:

2 cups sifted flour	½ teaspoon salt
2 eggs	2 tablespoons cold water

Sift the flour onto a board; make a well in the center. In it place the eggs, salt and water. Work in the flour with the fingers until a ball of dough is formed. If too dry, add a little more cold water. Scrape the board clean, and sprinkle with flour. Knead the dough until very smooth and elastic. Cover with a bowl and let rest 15 minutes while preparing the filling.

Filling:

1 cup ground cooked beef or chicken	¼ teaspoon minced garlic
¼ cup finely chopped ham	¼ teaspoon freshly ground black pepper
1 egg, beaten	½ teaspoon salt
¼ cup grated Parmesan cheese	

Mix together all the ingredients.

Divide the dough in 2 pieces. Roll out each piece paper-thin. Lift dough and sprinkle board and rolling pin with flour when necessary to keep it from sticking. Cut into strips 2-inches wide. At 2 inch intervals, place a teaspoon of filling. Cover with another strip of dough. Using the index finger, press gently around each mound. Cut into squares with a pastry wheel or knife. Be sure the edges are sealed. Let dry for 1 hour.

Cook in deep boiling salted water about 7 minutes, or until they rise to the surface. Drain and serve with melted butter and grated Parmesan cheese or with tomato sauce.

Makes about 30.

GNOCCHI di SEMOLINA

Semolina Dumplings

- 4 cups milk
- 1 teaspoon salt
- 1/8 teaspoon nutmeg
- 1 cup semolina or cream of wheat
- 4 egg, beaten
- 1 cup grated Romano or Parmesan cheese
- 5 tablespoons butter

Bring the milk, salt, and nutmeg to a boil. Very gradually stir in the semolina. Cook over low heat 10 minutes or until very thick. Stir frequently. Beat in the eggs, 2 tablespoons butter and ½ cup cheese. Pour into a buttered pan to a depth of ½ inch. Chill, then cut into 1½-inch squares. In a shallow buttered baking dish, arrange the squares in rows, slightly overlapping. Sprinkle with the remaining cheese and dot with the remaining butter. Bake in a preheated 400° oven 10 minutes or until browned.

Serves 4-6.

GNOCCHI di PATATE

Potato Dumplings

- 2 pounds potatoes
- 1 cup flour
- 3 egg yolks
- 2 teaspoons salt
- 1/4 teaspoon white pepper
- 1 tablespoon butter

Cook the potatoes in their skins until tender. Peel, and return to the saucepan. Shake over low heat until dry. Beat in an electric mixer or mash very smooth—it is important that no lumps remain. Mix in the flour, egg yolks, salt, pepper, and butter. Knead on a floured surface until smooth. If dough doesn't hold its shape, work in a little more flour. Break off portions of the dough and roll into long ¾-inch thick pieces. Cut into 1-inch lengths.

Drop singly into boiling salted water. Cook 10 minutes or until they rise to the surface. Remove with a slotted spoon. Serve with melted butter and grated cheese, or any sauce you like.

Serves 4-6.

GNOCCHI VERDE

Spinach-Cheese Dumplings

- 1 pound ricotta or cottage cheese
- 2 pounds spinach or 2 packages frozen, thawed
- 5 egg yolks
- 3 cups freshly grated Parmesan cheese
- ⅛ teaspoon nutmeg
- ¾ cup flour
- ½ cup melted butter

Press all the liquid from the ricotta or cottage cheese —it must be very dry.

Bring the spinach to a boil in salted water and drain thoroughly at once. Purée in an electric blender or chop very fine. Drain again if necessary.

Beat the egg yolks, then mix in the drained cheese, spinach, 2 cups Parmesan cheese, and the nutmeg. Beat well with a wooden spoon. Shape into balls and roll lightly in the flour.

Use a large deep skillet and almost fill it with water. Bring to a boil and reduce heat to low. Carefully add the dumplings one at a time. Cook over low heat until they rise to the surface. Drain well. Pour the melted butter over them and sprinkle with the remaining Parmesan cheese.

Serves 6-8.

RISI e BISI

Rice and Peas

- 4 tablespoons olive oil
- 4 tablespoons butter
- ¾ cup chopped onions
- 1½ cups raw rice
- 3 tablespoons Marsala or dry sherry
- 3 cups shelled peas or 2 packages frozen, thawed
- 3 cups hot chicken broth
- 1½ teaspoons salt
- ¼ teaspoon white pepper
- ¼ cup grated Parmesan cheese

Heat the oil and 2 tablespoons butter in a heavy saucepan; sauté the onions 5 minutes. Mix in the rice until translucent. Add the sherry, cook over low heat 1 minute. Add the peas, 2 cups broth, salt, and pepper. Cover, bring to a boil and cook over low heat 10 minutes. Add the remaining broth, recover and cook 10 minutes longer or until rice is tender and dry. Taste for seasoning; mix in the cheese and remaining butter.

Serves 6-8.

RISO alla GENOVESE

Rice, Genoa Style

- 3 tablespoons olive oil
- 1 cup chopped onions
- 1 cup chopped celery
- 1 cup grated carrots
- ½ pound ground veal
- 2½ teaspoons salt
- ½ teaspoon freshly ground black pepper
- ¼ teaspoon rosemary
- 2 tablespoon minced parsley
- ¾ cup dry white wine
- 3 cups water
- 1½ cups raw rice
- 2 tablespoons butter

Heat the oil in a saucepan; sauté the onions, celery, and carrots 10 minutes. Mix in the veal, 1 teaspoon salt, the pepper, rosemary, and parsley; sauté 5 minutes, stirring frequently. Add the wine; cover and cook over low heat 50 minutes.

Meanwhile cook the rice. Combine the water, rice, and remaining salt in a saucepan; bring to a boil, cover and cook over low heat 15 minutes. Drain, if any water remains. Put in a clean saucepan and shake over low heat to dry. Mix in the butter and half the sauce; cook over low heat 5 minutes, stirring almost constantly. Transfer to a hot serving dish and cover with the remaining sauce. Serve with grated Parmesan cheese.

Serves 4-6.

RISO VERDE

Green Rice

2 tablespoons olive oil	2 cups raw rice
4 tablespoons butter	3½ cups hot chicken broth
1 cup minced scallions (green onions)	1½ teaspoons salt
	¼ teaspoon white pepper
1 cup minced parsley	Grated Parmesan cheese
1½ cup finely chopped raw spinach	

Heat the oil and 2 tablespoons butter in a heavy saucepan; mix in the scallions, parsley, and spinach. Cover and cook over low heat 5 minutes. Mix in the rice until translucent. Add 2 cups broth, the salt and pepper; cover and cook over low heat 20 minutes, adding the remaining broth after 10 minutes. Lightly mix in the remaining butter with a fork. Serve with the cheese.

Serves 4-6.

RISOTTO SPECIALE

Special Rice Dish

6 tablespoons butter	¼ pound chicken livers, diced
¾ cup finely chopped onions	½ pound mushrooms, sliced
2 cups raw rice	1 cup beef broth
⅓ cup Marsala or sweet sherry	1 teaspoon salt
5 cups hot chicken broth	¼ teaspoon freshly ground black pepper
1½ teaspoons salt	1 bay leaf
½ cup thinly sliced onions	¼ teaspoon thyme
½ cup julienne-cut prosciutto ham	

Melt half the butter in a saucepan; sauté the chopped onions until yellow and transparent. Stir in the rice until lightly browned. Add ¼ cup wine; cook until absorbed. Add 2 cups broth and the salt; cover and cook over low heat 25 minutes, adding the remaining chicken broth as it becomes absorbed by the rice. Meanwhile prepare the sauce.

Melt the remaining butter in a small saucepan; sauté the sliced onion and ham 5 minutes. Add the livers and mushrooms; sauté 5 minutes, stirring frequently. Mix in the beef broth, salt, pepper, bay leaf, thyme, and remaining wine. Cook over low heat 10 minutes. Taste for seasoning. Discard the bay leaf, then mix half the sauce with the rice. Heap in a bowl and pour remaining sauce over the top.

Serves 4-6.

POLENTA PASTICCIATA

Corn Meal Pie

1 quart water	⅛ teaspoon nutmeg
3 teaspoons salt	3 cups milk
1 cup yellow corn meal	¾ cup grated Parmesan cheese
6 tablespoons butter	
3 tablespoons flour	¾ pound mushrooms, thinly sliced
¼ teaspoon white pepper	

Bring the water and 2 tablespoons salt to a boil; stir in the corn meal until it begins to thicken. Cook over low heat 20 minutes, stirring frequently.

Melt 4 tablespoons butter in a skillet; blend in the flour, pepper, nutmeg, and ½ teaspoon salt. Add the milk, stirring steadily to the boiling point. Cook over low heat 15 minutes. Mix in ½ cup cheese until melted.

Sauté the mushrooms in the remaining butter 5 minutes. Season with the remaining salt.

In a buttered shallow baking dish, spread ⅓ the corn meal, then ⅓ the sauce and ⅓ the mushrooms. Repeat the layers twice more ending with the sauce. Sprinkle with the remaining cheese. Bake in a 375° oven 30 minutes or until browned.

Serves 6-8.

POLENTA al FORMAGGIO

Corn Meal and Cheese

1 quart water	2 cups grated Gruyère or Swiss cheese
1½ teaspoon salt	
1 cup yellow corn meal	6 tablespoons butter

Bring the water and salt to a boil; stir in the corn meal until it begins to thicken. Cook over low heat 20 minutes, stirring frequently.

Spread half the corn meal on the bottom of a shallow

buttered baking dish; cover with half the cheese and dot with half the butter. Repeat the layers. Bake in a 375° oven 15 minutes or until browned.

Serves 4-6.

SALSA alla GENOVESE

Meat Sauce, Genoa Style

3 dried mushrooms	2 cups peeled chopped tomatoes
3 tablespoons butter	
¾ cup chopped onions	1½ teaspoons salt
¼ cup grated carrots	½ teaspoon freshly ground black pepper
¼ cup chopped celery	
½ cup ground veal	¾ cup dry white wine
2 tablespoons flour	1½ cups chicken broth

Wash the mushrooms, cover with warm water and let soak 15 minutes. Drain, and slice fine.

Melt the butter in a saucepan; sauté the onions, carrots, and celery 5 minutes. Add the veal and mushrooms; cook over medium heat until browned, stirring almost constantly. Blend in the flour, then the tomatoes; cook 3 minutes. Stir in the salt, pepper, wine, and broth. Cover and cook over low heat 45 minutes. Taste for seasoning. Serve with pasta.

Makes about 3 cups.

SUGO di CARNE, I

Meat Sauce

1 pound ground beef	¾ cup dry red wine
2 tablespoons flour	1½ cups canned Italian-style tomatoes
4 tablespoons olive oil	
¾ cup chopped onions	1½ cups beef broth
¼ cup grated carrots	¾ cup chopped mushrooms
1 tablespoon minced parsley	1½ teaspoons salt
½ teaspoon freshly ground black pepper	

Toss the beef with the flour. Heat the oil in a saucepan; sauté the onions, carrots and parsley 10 minutes. Add the beef; cook until no red remains, stirring frequently to prevent lumps from forming. Add the wine; cook over high heat 3 minutes. Mix in the tomatoes, broth, mushrooms, salt, and pepper. Cook over low heat 1½ hours. Taste for seasoning.

Makes about 3 cups.

SUGO di CARNE, II

Meat Sauce

3 dried mushrooms	1 tablespoon flour
2 tablespoons butter	1½ teaspoons salt
¾ cup chopped onions	½ teaspoon freshly ground black pepper
½ cup grated carrots	
3 tablespoons minced parsley	2 teaspoons tomato paste
¾ pound ground beef	½ cup dry white wine
2 cups beef broth	

Wash the mushrooms, cover with water, and let soak 15 minutes. Drain and slice fine.

Melt the butter in a saucepan; sauté the onions, carrots, and parsley 5 minutes. Add the meat and mushrooms; cook over medium heat, stirring almost constantly until browned. Blend in the flour, salt, and pepper, then the tomato paste. Add the wine and broth. Cook over low heat 45 minutes, stirring frequently. Taste for seasoning. Serve with pasta.

Makes about 3 cups.

RAGU, I

Bolognese Sauce

- 2 tablespoons butter
- ¼ pound ham, cut julienne
- ¾ cup chopped onions
- ¼ cup chopped celery
- ½ cup grated carrots
- ¾ pound ground beef
- ½ pound chicken livers, diced
- 1½ tablespoons tomato paste
- ¾ cup dry white wine
- 1½ cups water
- 1 teaspoon salt
- ½ teaspoon freshly ground black pepper
- ⅛ teaspoon nutmeg

Melt the butter in a saucepan; sauté the ham, onions, celery, and carrots 10 minutes, stirring frequently. Add the beef; cook over medium heat, stirring almost constantly, until browned. Stir in the livers for 2 minutes. Blend in the tomato paste, then stir in the wine, water, salt, pepper, and nutmeg. Cover and cook over low heat 45 minutes, stirring frequently. Taste for seasoning. Serve with pastas. For a richer sauce, add 1 cup heavy cream before mixing with the pasta.

Makes about 3 cups.

RAGU, II

Bolognese Sauce

- 6 tablespoons butter
- 1 cup finely chopped onions
- ½ cup grated carrots
- 1 pound ground beef
- 1 8-ounce can tomato sauce
- 4 cups beef broth or water
- 1½ teaspoons salt
- ½ teaspoon freshly ground black pepper
- 1 cup heavy cream

Melt the butter in a saucepan; sauté the onions and carrots 10 minutes. Add the beef; cook, stirring frequently, until no pink remains. Add the tomato sauce, broth, salt, and pepper; cover and cook over low heat 2 hours, stirring occasionally. Mix in the cream and taste for seasoning.

Serves 6-8.

SALSA di POMODORO

Fresh Tomato Sauce

4 tablespoons butter	2 teaspoons salt
½ cup chopped onions	½ teaspoon freshly ground
¼ cup grated carrots	black pepper
¼ cup chopped celery	⅛ teaspoon sugar
2 tablespoons minced parsley	½ teaspoon basil

2 pounds very ripe tomatoes, chopped

Melt the butter in a saucepan; sauté the onions, carrots, celery, and parsley 5 minutes. Add the tomatoes, salt, pepper, sugar, and basil. Bring to a boil and cook over low heat 45 minutes. Purée in an electric blender or force through a sieve. Use as directed in recipes, or serve with pasta.

Makes about 2½ cups.

SALSA di FEGATINI

Chicken Liver Sauce

5 dried mushrooms	¼ teaspoon freshly ground
1 pound chicken livers	black pepper
3 tablespoons flour	⅓ cup Marsala or sweet
4 tablespoons butter	sherry
1 teaspoon salt	1½ cups chicken broth

2 tablespoons minced parsley

Wash the mushrooms, cover with warm water and let soak 15 minutes. Drain and chop.

Wash the livers, remove any discolored areas and dry. Dice the livers and toss with the flour.

Melt the butter in a saucepan; sauté the livers and mushrooms 5 minutes. Season with the salt and pepper and add the wine; cook over medium heat 3 minutes. Add the broth; cook over low heat 20 minutes. Mix in the parsley and taste for seasoning. Serve with pasta, but particularly good with *Gnocchi* (see recipe).

Makes about 2½ cups.

Chapter 7

Poultry

POLLO alla PIEMONTESE

Chicken, Piedmont Style

½ cup olive oil
2 tablespoons lemon juice
¼ cup minced onion
2 tablespoons minced parsley
1½ teaspoons salt
1 3-pound frying chicken, disjointed
¾ cup sifted flour
½ cup water
1 egg white

Mix together ¼ cup oil, the lemon juice, onion, parsley, and half the salt. Rub into the chicken very well and let stand 2 hours. Prepare the batter meanwhile.

Beat together the flour, water, and remaining salt and oil. Let stand 1 hour. Beat the egg white until stiff and fold into the batter. Dip the chicken in it, coating them well. Arrange on a greased baking pan. Bake in a 425° oven 45 minutes, turning the pieces once.

Serves 4.

POLLO alla FIORENTINA

Fried Marinated Chicken

3-pound fryer, disjointed
2 tablespoons lemon juice
¼ cup olive oil
1½ teaspoons salt
½ teaspoon freshly ground black pepper
½ cup flour
2 eggs, beaten
1 tablespoon milk
1½ cups olive or vegetable oil

Wash and dry the chicken. Marinate for 4 hours in a mixture of the lemon juice, ¼ cup olive oil, salt, and pepper. Baste and turn frequently. Remove the chicken parts and dry with paper towels. Roll in the flour, then dip in the eggs beaten with the milk.

Heat the 1½ cups oil in a skillet until it bubbles. Brown the chicken in it on all sides. Cover loosely and cook over low heat 15 minutes or until tender. Drain on absorbent paper.

Serves 4.

POLLA alla DIAVOLO

Deviled Broiled Chicken

2 2-pound broilers, split	5 tablespoons olive oil
2 teaspoons salt	½ cup finely chopped onions
½ teaspoon crushed dried red peppers	2 tablespoons minced parsley
	½ cup dry vermouth

Wash and dry the broilers, rub with the salt and red peppers. Brush with the oil. Place in a broiling pan skin side down. Broil 4 inches from the heat 20 minutes. Turn skin side up and broil 20 minutes longer, adding a mixture of the onions and parsley after 10 minutes. Transfer the chickens to a serving dish. Place the broiling pan over direct heat. Add the vermouth, bring to a boil, scraping the pan of all browned particles. Cook 1 minute and pour over the broilers.

Serves 4.

POLLO alla ROMANA

Chicken, Roman Style

3½ pound fryer, disjointed	2 tablespoons olive oil
2 teaspoons salt	1 clove garlic, minced
½ teaspoon freshly ground black pepper	¼ teaspoon rosemary
2 slices bacon, diced	½ cup dry white wine
2 tablespoons butter	2 teaspoons tomato paste
	½ cup chicken broth

Wash and dry the chicken pieces rub with the salt and pepper. In a Dutch oven or heavy frying pan, brown the bacon. Pour off the fat; add the butter and oil and heat. Add the chicken and garlic. Sauté until browned. Mix in the rosemary and wine. Cook over low heat 15 minutes. Mix the tomato paste and broth; add to the chicken. Cover and cook over low heat 30 minutes or until chicken is tender.

Serves 4.

FEGATINI di POLLO

Chicken Livers in Wine Sauce

1 pound chicken livers	¼ teaspoon freshly ground black pepper
4 slices bacon, diced	
4 tablespoons butter	⅛ teaspoon sage
1¼ teaspoons salt	½ cup Marsala or sweet sherry

Wash the livers and remove any discolored spots; cut each half in two.

In a skillet, lightly brown the bacon; pour off the fat. Add the butter to the skillet, and when melted, the livers. Sauté 2 minutes; season with the salt, pepper, and sage. Sauté 2 minutes longer. Remove and keep hot.

Stir the wine into the skillet. scraping the bottom of browned particles. Cook over medium heat 1 minute. Pour over the livers. The livers may be served on sautéed bread, if you like.

Serves 4.

COSTOLETTE di POLLO

Chicken Breasts with Cheese Sauce

- 3 whole chicken breasts
- 1½ teaspoons salt
- ¼ teaspoon white pepper
- 3 tablespoons flour
- 4 tablespoons butter
- ½ cup milk
- 3 tablespoons grated Parmesan cheese
- 2 tablespoons grated Swiss cheese

Cut the chicken breasts in half through the breast bone. Remove the skin and bones. Place between 2 sheets of waxed paper and pound very thin. Rub with a mixture of the salt, pepper and 2 tablespoons flour.

Melt 3 tablespoons butter in a skillet; brown the chicken in it. Transfer to a shallow baking dish.

Melt 1 tablespoon butter in a saucepan; blend in remaining flour. Gradually add the milk, stirring steadily to the boiling point; cook over low heat 5 minutes. Mix in the cheeses until melted. Spread over the chicken. Bake in a preheated 370° oven 10 minutes or until browned.

Serves 6.

PETTI di POLLO al PROSCIUTTO

Breast of Chicken, Milan Style

- 3 whole chicken breasts
- ¼ cup flour
- 1½ teaspoons salt
- ¼ teaspoon white pepper
- 2 tablespoons butter
- 2 tablespoons olive oil
- 6 sage leaves or ½ teaspoon dried
- 6 slices prosciutto ham
- ½ cup dry white wine

Cut the chicken breasts in half through the breast bone. Remove the skin and bones. Place between 2 sheets of waxed paper and pound very thin. Dip in a mixture of the flour, salt, and pepper.

Heat the butter and oil in a skillet; sauté the chicken breasts until browned on the under side. Turn over and place a sage leaf on each or sprinkle with the dried sage. Cover with the ham. Sauté 5 minutes. Add the wine; bring to a boil and cook over low heat 2 minutes. Transfer chicken to a heated serving dish. Scrape the pan and pour the juices over the chicken.

Serves 6.

FILETTO di POLLO alla BOLOGNESE

Breast of Chicken and Ham

3 whole chicken breasts	6 tablespoons butter
2 eggs, beaten	6 slices prosciutto or cooked ham
1½ teaspoons salt	
¼ teaspoon white pepper	1 cup grated Parmesan cheese
½ cup flour	½ cup chicken broth

Cut the breasts in half through the breast bone. Remove the skin and bones. Place between 2 sheets of waxed paper and pound thin. Dip in a mixture of the eggs, salt and pepper, then the flour.

Melt the butter in a skillet; brown the chicken on both sides. Place a slice of ham on each chicken piece and cover with grated cheese. Add the broth, cover and cook over low heat 5 minutes.

Serves 6.

Note: Slices of raw turkey breast may be prepared in the same manner.

FRICASSE di POLLO

Chicken Fricassee

1 3½-pound fryer, disjointed	½ cup dry white wine
2 tablespoons flour	1 cup peeled diced tomatoes
2 teaspoons salt	⅛ teaspoon rosemary
½ teaspoon freshly ground black pepper	2 tablespoons minced parsley
	¼ pound mushrooms, sliced
¼ cup olive oil	2 tablespoons butter
1 clove garlic, minced	

Rub the chicken with a mixture of the flour, salt and pepper. Heat the oil in a heavy skillet; brown the chicken in it. Add the garlic, wine, tomatoes, rosemary, and parsley. Cover and cook over low heat 20 minutes or until the chicken is tender. Sauté the mushrooms in the butter while the chicken is cooking. Add to the chicken just before serving.

Serves 4.

POLLO NOVELLO e PEPERONI

Chicken and Peppers, Umbrian Style

1 pullet, disjointed	2 cups chopped tomatoes
2 teaspoons salt	1 cup chicken broth
½ teaspoon freshly ground black pepper	¼ cup grated Romano or Parmesan cheese
4 tablespoons butter	3 peppers (green and red) in narrow strips
1 clove garlic, minced	
¾ cup minced onions	3 tablespoons olive oil
3 tablespoons butter	2 tablespoons minced parsley

Season the chicken with salt and pepper. Sauté the onions and garlic in the butter 10 minutes. Add the chicken; cook until browned. Add the tomatoes and broth. Cover and cook over low heat 40 minutes. Remove the chicken and stir the cheese into the gravy. Taste for seasoning.

While the chicken is cooking, sauté the peppers in the olive oil. Add to the chicken 20 minutes before it is finished. Sprinkle with the parsley.

Serves 4.

POLLO ARROSTO

Roast Stuffed Chicken

5-pound capon or roasting chicken	3 tablespoons olive oil
¼ teaspoon thyme	½ cup chopped onions
3 teaspoons salt	2 cups soft bread crumbs
¾ teaspoon freshly ground black pepper	¼ tablespoon grated Parmesan cheese
	2 eggs, beaten
3 tablespoons butter	

Wash and dry the chicken, liver, heart, and gizzards. Chop the giblets very fine. Rub the chicken with a mixture of the thyme, 2 teaspoons salt and ½ teaspoon pepper.

Heat the oil in a skillet; sauté the onions 5 minutes. Add the giblets; sauté 10 minutes. Mix in the bread crumbs thoroughly, then the parsley, cheese, eggs, and remaining salt and pepper. Taste for seasoning and cool.

Stuff the chicken, closing the opening with skewers. Place in a buttered shallow roasting pan and dot with butter.

Roast in a 375° oven 2 hours or until tender and browned, basting frequently with the pan drippings.

Serves 4-5.

POLLO alla ROMANA

Chicken, Roman Style

5-pound capon or roasting chicken, disjointed	4 tablespoons butter
¼ cup flour	½ cup finely chopped onions
2 teaspoons salt	¼ cup julienne-cut ham
½ teaspoon freshly ground black pepper	⅓ cup dry white wine
	1½ cups peeled chopped tomatoes
¼ teaspoon rosemary	

Rub the chicken pieces with a mixture of the flour, salt and pepper. Melt 2 tablespoons butter in a skillet with ovenproof handle); brown the chicken in it. Remove. Melt the remaining butter in the skillet; sauté the onions and ham 5 minutes. Return the chicken and add the wine and rosemary; cook over low heat until wine is absorbed. Add the tomatoes. Cover and bake in a 350° oven 1 hour or until chicken is tender. Taste for seasoning.

Serves 4-5.

Variation: Pollo alla Romano con Peperoni

15 minutes before chicken is tender, add 2 sliced sautéed green peppers and 1 clove minced garlic.

CAPPONE ARROSTO
Roast Capon with Caper Sauce

5-pound capon	3 cups chicken broth
1 tablespoon salt	2 tablespoons butter
½ teaspoon freshly ground black pepper	2 tablespoons flour
	1 egg yolk
3 tablespoons warm cognac	1 cup heavy cream
1 tablespoon chopped capers	

Wash and dry the capon; rub with a mixture of the salt and pepper. Place in a shallow buttered roasting pan; roast in a 400° oven 20 minutes. Pour the cognac over it and set aflame; when flames die, add the broth. Reduce heat to 350° and roast 1½ hours longer, or until tender, basting frequently. Pour off the pan juices and reserve.

Melt the butter in a saucepan; blend in the flour. Add the pan juices, stirring constantly to the boiling point; cook over low heat 5 minutes. Beat the egg yolk and cream in a bowl; gradually add the hot sauce, stirring steadily to prevent curdling. Return to saucepan; cook over low heat, stirring steadily, until thickened, but do not let boil. Mix in the capers and taste for seasoning.

Carve the capon and pour sauce over it.

Serves 4-5.

CROCCHETTE di POLLO con PROSCIUTTO

Chicken-Ham Croquettes

- 2 tablespoons butter
- 2 tablespoons flour
- ¾ cup light cream
- 2 tablespoons grated Parmesan cheese
- 1½ cups chopped cooked chicken
- 1 cup chopped cooked ham
- 2 egg yolks, beaten
- 1 teaspoon salt
- ¼ teaspoon white pepper
- ¾ cup fine bread crumbs
- Vegetable oil for deep frying

Melt the butter in a saucepan; blend in the flour. Add the cream, stirring steadily to the boiling point; cook over low heat 10 minutes. The sauce should be very thick. Remove from the heat and stir in the cheese. Cool, then mix in the chicken, ham, egg yolks, salt, and pepper. Taste for seasoning and chill 3 hours.

Shape the mixture into 6-8 croquettes. Roll in the bread crumbs. Heat the fat to 370° and fry the croquettes until browned. Drain.

Serves 3-4.

TACCHINO FILETTO di con FORMAGGIO

Turkey Rolls

- 1 whole turkey breast
- ¼ cup flour
- 2 teaspoons salt
- ¼ teaspoon white pepper
- 6 thin slices prosciutto or cooked ham
- 6 thin slices mozzarella or Swiss cheese
- 6 cooked asparagus tips
- 6 tablespoons butter
- ½ cup Marsala or sweet sherry
- ¼ cup chicken broth

94 / Cook as the Romans Do

Have the turkey breast cut in half through the breast bone. Remove the skin and bones. Cut each breast half into 3 thin fillets. Pound each as thin as possible. Dip the fillets in a mixture of the flour, salt, and pepper. Place a slice of ham on each, then a slice of cheese and an asparagus. Roll up carefully and tie with thread or fasten with toothpicks.

Melt 4 tablespoons butter in a skillet; sauté the rolls over very low heat until tender and browned. Transfer to a heated serving dish. To the skillet, add the wine, broth, and remaining butter. Bring to a boil, scraping the pan of browned particles. Pour over the rolls.

Serves 6.

Note: Chicken breasts may be prepared in the same manner.

TACCHINO RIPIENO
Stuffed Turkey

12-pound turkey
1 tablespoon salt
½ teaspoon freshly ground black pepper
1½ pounds chestnuts
2 tablespoons olive oil
¼ pound ground veal
¼ pound ground beef
1 Italian sausage, chopped
½ cup chopped onions
1 clove garlic, minced
½ cup chopped prunes
½ cup dry white wine
½ cup grated Parmesan cheese
⅛ teaspoon thyme
2 eggs, beaten
4 tablespoons melted butter
1 onion, sliced
1 bay leaf
2 cups water

Wash and dry the turkey. Rub inside and out with the salt and pepper.

Make a crisscross cut in the pointed end of the chestnuts. Cover with water, bring to a boil and cook over low heat 20 minutes. Drain, cool and remove the shells and inner skin. Chop coarsely.

Heat the oil in a skillet; sauté the veal, beef, sausage, onions, and garlic 5 minutes, stirring almost constantly. Remove from the heat; mix in the prunes, wine, cheese, thyme, eggs, and chestnuts. Cool, then stuff the turkey. Close the opening with skewers or aluminum foil. Place in a roasting pan and brush with the butter. Add the sliced onion and bay leaf. Roast in a 350° oven 1 hour. Add 1 cup water; roast 1½ hours longer or until tender, basting frequently. Add the remaining water from time to time. Transfer to a heated platter and serve with the strained pan juices.

Serves 12-14.

ANITRA all'OLIVE

Duck with Olive Sauce

6-pound duck	½ cup finely chopped onions
2 teaspoons salt	½ cup grated carrots
½ teaspoon freshly ground black pepper	2 cups dry red wine
	1 bay leaf
½ teaspoon thyme	1½ cups pitted green olives

Wash the duck, remove as much fat as possible and dry. Rub inside and out with a mixture of the salt, pepper, and thyme. In a Dutch oven or heavy casserole, brown the duck on all sides. Pour off the fat. Add the onions and carrots; cook 10 minutes. Add the wine, and bay leaf. Bring to a boil. Cover and cook over low heat 1¼ hours or until tender. Baste frequently. Drain duck and place on a heated serving dish.

Skim the fat off the gravy, then strain. Pour into a saucepan and add the olives; cook 5 minutes. Carve the duck and pour the sauce over it.

Serves 4.

ANITRA in AGRODOLCE

Duck in Sweet and Sour Sauce

5-6 pound duck, disjointed	1½ cups thinly sliced onions
½ cup flour	1½ cups boiling water
2 teaspoons salt	½ cup dry white wine
½ teaspoon freshly ground black pepper	⅛ teaspoon ground cloves
	4 tablespoons sugar
2 tablespoons butter	3 tablespoons water
3 tablespoons wine vinegar	

Remove as much fat as possible from the duck, wash and dry. Roll in a mixture of the flour, salt, and pepper.

Melt the butter in a Dutch oven or heavy casserole; brown the duck and onions in it. Pour off the fat. Add the boiling water, wine, and cloves; cover and cook over low heat 1½ hours, or until tender. Shake the pan and turn the pieces frequently. Remove the duck; skim the fat from the gravy.

Cook the sugar and 3 tablespoons water until it turns caramel color; stir into the gravy with the vinegar. Cook 5 minutes. Taste for seasoning. Serve in a sauceboat.

Serves 4.

PICCIONI con PISELLI

Squab with Peas

4 squabs	¼ pound ham, cut julienne
1 tablespoon salt	¾ cup dry white wine
¾ teaspoons freshly ground black pepper	¾ cup boiling water
	1 pound green peas, shelled or 1 package frozen, thawed
½ teaspoon basil	
3 tablespoons butter	¼ pound chicken livers, diced and sautéed
1 cup chopped onions	

Wash and dry the squabs; rub inside and out with a mixture of the salt, pepper, and basil. Melt the butter in a Dutch oven or deep heavy skillet; sauté the onions 10 minutes. Add the squabs; brown on all sides. Mix in the ham and wine; cook over medium heat 5 minutes. Add the water, cover, and cook over low heat 30 minutes. Add the peas; recover and cook 15 minutes. Mix in the livers; cook 5 minutes longer. Taste for seasoning. Transfer the squabs to a serving dish and pour gravy over all.

Serves 4.

TACCHINO STUFATO

Turkey Fricassee

- 6-8 pound turkey, cut in serving-size pieces
- ½ cup flour
- 2½ teaspoons salt
- ¾ teaspoon freshly ground black pepper
- 4 tablespoons butter
- 1 cup chopped onions
- 1 slice ham, julienne-cut
- ½ teaspoon marjoram
- 2 tablespoons minced parsley
- 1 bay leaf
- 2 slices lemon
- 1½ cup dry white wine
- 2 cups boiling water
- ¼ cup dry bread crumbs
- ½ pound mushrooms, sliced and sautéed

Wash and dry the turkey pieces. Rub with a mixture of the flour, salt, and pepper.

Melt the butter in a Dutch oven or heavy casserole; sauté the onions 10 minutes. Add the turkey pieces and brown on all sides. Mix in the ham, marjoram, parsley, bay leaf, lemon, and wine. Bring to a boil and cook 10 minutes. Add the water. Cover and cook over low heat 1¼ hours or until tender. Remove the turkey and keep hot. Strain the gravy into a saucepan pressing through as much as possible. Stir in the bread crumbs until smooth, then the mushrooms; cook over low heat 15 minutes. Taste for seasoning and pour over the turkey.

Serves 8-10.

Note: Chicken may be prepared in the same manner.

TEGAMINO

Sweetbreads and Chicken Livers Casserole

- 3 pairs sweetbreads
- 1 tablespoon vinegar
- 1 pound chicken livers
- 6 tablespoons butter
- 2 teaspoons salt
- ½ teaspoon freshly ground black pepper
- ¾ cup dry white wine
- ½ pound mushrooms, sliced and sautéed
- 1½ cups cooked green peas

Wash the sweetbreads and soak in cold water 10 minutes. Drain, add fresh water to cover and the vinegar. Bring to a boil and cook over low heat 15 minutes. Drain and cover with cold water; let stand 15 minutes. Drain, remove membrane, and cut each part in half crosswise. Wash the livers, removing any discolored areas.

Spread a tablespoon of butter in 6 shallow casseroles or ramekins. Put 2 pieces of sweetbread in each. Divide the livers among them. Season with the salt and pepper and add 2 tablespoons of wine to each. Bake in 425° oven 10 minutes. Divide the mushrooms and peas among the casseroles; reduce heat to 350° and bake 5 minutes longer.

Serves 6.

Chapter 8

Meats

FILETTO al VERMOUTH

Fillet of Beef with Vermouth Sauce

4 fillets of beef, cut 1-inch thick	¾ teaspoon salt
2 tablespoons butter	¼ teaspoon freshly ground black pepper
½ cup sliced green olives	¼ cup dry vermouth
¼ cup heavy cream	

Don't have any fat wrapped around the meat. Melt the butter in a skillet; add the fillets and olives. Cook over high heat 2 minutes on each side, shaking the pan a few times. Sprinkle the meat with the salt and pepper. Add the vermouth and cream. Cook over low heat 4 minutes longer, or to desired degree of rareness.

Arrange the fillets on a hot serving dish and pour the sauce over them.

Serves 4.

FILETTO al PATE

Fillet of Beef with Pâté

6 fillets of beef, cut 1½-inches thick	2 tablespoons olive oil
1½ teaspoons salt	2 tablespoons butter
½ teaspoon freshly ground black pepper	¼ cup Marsala or sweet sherry
¼ cup warm cognac	4-ounce can pate de foie gras

Season the fillets with the salt and pepper and rub with the oil. Let stand at room temperature 1 hour.

Melt the butter in a skillet; cook the fillets over high

heat 1 minute on each side, or until browned. Remove. Add the wine and pâté to the skillet. Cook over low heat, stirring constantly until smooth. Return the fillets; cook 2 minutes. Pour the cognac over them and set aflame; shake the pan until flames die. Transfer steaks to a serving dish and pour the sauce over them.

Serves 4.

FILETTO RIPIENO

Stuffed Fillets

- 6 fillets of beef, cut ¾-inch thick
- 6 slices prosciutto or cooked ham
- 6 thin slices mozzarella or Swiss cheese
- 1 teaspoon salt
- ¼ teaspoon freshly ground black pepper
- ⅓ cup flour
- 2 eggs, beaten
- ½ cup dry bread crumbs
- 5 tablespoons butter

Cut the steaks horizontally through the middle, leaving one side attached. Open like a book. Put a slice of ham and a slice of cheese on each, then close up, pressing the edges together firmly. Season with the salt and pepper, dip in the flour, the eggs, and finally the bread crumbs.

Melt the butter in a skillet; sauté the steaks 5 minutes on each side, or to desired degree of rareness.

Serves 6.

MANZO RIPIENO

Stuffed Beef

- 1 flank steak
- 2 slices white bread
- ½ cup water
- ¼ pound chicken livers, diced
- ¾ cup chopped onions
- ¼ cup chopped celery
- ¼ cup minced parsley
- ¼ cup grated Parmesan cheese
- ¼ pound cooked ham, cut julienne
- 1 egg, beaten
- 2½ teaspoons salt
- ¾ teaspoon freshly ground black pepper
- ¾ teaspoon oregano
- 3 tablespoons olive oil
- 2 cups water

Have the steak pounded very thin. Soak the bread in the water 10 minutes; drain and mash smooth. Combine with the livers, onions, celery, parsley, cheese, ham, egg, 1 teaspoon salt, ½ teaspoon pepper, and ⅓ teaspoon oregano. Spread on the steak; roll up and tie with string.

Heat the oil in a Dutch oven or heavy deep skillet; brown the roll in it. Sprinkle with the remaining salt, pepper, and oregano; add the water. Cover and cook over low heat 2 hours or until tender. Serve warm (meat should stand at room temperature for 20 minutes for easier slicing) or cold.

Serves 4-6.

COSTA di MANZO al VINO ROSSO
Marinated Roast Beef

- 2-3 lb rib roast
- 3 cups dry red wine
- ¾ cup sliced onions
- ½ cup sliced carrots
- 2 cloves garlic, minced
- 2 bay leaves
- ½ teaspoon freshly ground black pepper
- 2½ teaspoons salt

Have the bones cut down very short (use for soup or braising). Have the trimmed meat weighed. Put the meat in a bowl (not metal). Pour the wine over it, and add the onions, carrots, garlic, bay leaves, and pepper. Marinate in the refrigerator 24 hours, basting and turning the meat several times.

Drain (reserve marinade) and dry the meat with paper towels; rub with the salt. Place in a shallow roasting pan; roast in a 450° oven 20 minutes. Meanwhile, cook the marinade until reduced to half. Pour over the meat; roast 15 minutes to a pound, basting frequently.

Serves 4-8.

STUFATINO alla ROMANA

Beef Stew, Roman Style

3 pounds eye round, cross rib, etc.	2 slices bacon, diced
2 teaspoons salt	2 tablespoons butter
½ teaspoon freshly ground black pepper	1 cup thinly sliced onions
	2 cloves garlic, minced
½ teaspoon marjoram	1 cup dry red wine
	1 tablespoon tomato paste
1 cup boiling water	

Cut the meat in ¾-inch thick slices; season with the salt, pepper and marjoram. In a Dutch oven or heavy casserole, lightly brown the bacon. Pour off half the fat. Add the butter, onions, and garlic; sauté 5 minutes. Add the meat; cook over medium heat until browned on both sides. Stir in the wine; cook until reduced to half. Blend in the tomato paste, then the water. Cover and cook over low heat 1½ hours. Taste for seasoning.

Serves 6-8.

BUE alla MODA del LOMBARDIA

Beef in Spicy Sauce

4 pounds cross rib or rump of beef	½ cup sliced carrots
	¼ cup wine vinegar
2½ teaspoons salt	1½ cups dry white wine
½ teaspoon freshly ground black pepper	1½ pounds tomatoes, peeled and diced
1 clove garlic, minced	2 bay leaves
2 tablespoons butter	¼ teaspoon sugar
1 cup thinly sliced onions	¼ cup heavy cream

Rub the meat with the salt, pepper, and garlic. Melt the butter in a Dutch oven or heavy saucepan; add the meat, onions, and carrots. Cook over medium heat until meat browns on all sides. Add the vinegar, wine, tomatoes, bay leaves, and sugar. Cover and cook over low heat 2½ hours or until meat is tender. Taste for seasoning.

Pour off the gravy and discard the bay leaves. Purée the gravy in an electric blender or force through a sieve. If too thin, cook over high heat a few minutes. Stir in the cream. Slice the beef and pour gravy over it.

Serves 6-8.

STUFATO di MANZO alla GENOVESE

Beef with White Wine

3 pounds eye round, cross rib etc.	¾ cup sliced carrots
	¼ cup sliced celery
4 tablespoons butter	2 teaspoons salt
3 cups thinly sliced onions	½ teaspoon freshly ground black pepper
1½ cups peeled diced tomatoes	½ teaspoon basil
1 cup dry white wine	

Rinse the meat and pat dry. Melt the butter in a Dutch oven or heavy skillet; sauté the onions until soft and yellow. Add the meat and brown it on all sides. Add the tomatoes, carrots, celery, salt, pepper, basil, and wine. Bring to a boil, cover and cook over low heat 2 hours or until the meat is tender. Slice the meat and serve with the gravy.

Serves 6-8.

MANZO BRASATO

Braised Beef in Red Wine

4 pounds eye round, cross rib or rump of beef	2 cloves garlic, minced
	2 teaspoons salt
4 tablespoons olive oil	½ teaspoon freshly ground black pepper
1 tablespoon butter	½ teaspoon rosemary
2 cups dry red wine	1 bay leaf
1½ cups chopped onions	Dash ground cloves
½ cup grated carrots	1½ cups diced tomatoes
½ cup diced celery	

Have the beef larded or do it yourself. Put all the ingredients in a Dutch oven or heavy saucepan. Cover tightly; bring to a boil and cook over low heat 2½ hours or until tender. Transfer the meat to a baking pan; purée the vegetables in an electric blender or force through a sieve. Pour over the meat. Bake in a 450° oven 15 minutes.

Serves 6-8.

ABBACCHIO al FORNO

Roast Leg of Lamb

3- to 4-pound leg of lamb	½ teaspoon freshly ground black pepper
3 cloves garlic, cut in slivers	
8 rosemary leaves or ½ teaspoon, dried	4 tablespoons butter
2 teaspoons salt	1½ cups dry white wine

In Italy, Abbacchio is newly born milk-fed lamb. Our hot house or baby lamb is not so young, but makes a good substitute. Make a few slits in the leg, and into them insert some garlic and rosemary. Rub the leg with the salt and pepper. Place in a shallow roasting pan and dot with the butter. Roast in a 450° oven 25 minutes or until browned. Pour off the fat. Add the wine; reduce heat to 350° and roast 1 hour longer or until tender; baste frequently.

Serves 4-6.

ABBACCHIO MARINATO

Marinated Roast Lamb

4-5 pound leg of lamb	1 teaspoon rosemary
1 tablespoon salt	½ cup olive oil
¾ teaspoon freshly ground black pepper	⅓ cup wine vinegar

Remove the fell (skin) of the lamb and trim the fat. Prick the lamb in several places, then rub with the salt, pepper and rosemary. Place in a bowl, and pour over the oil mixed with the vinegar. Marinate in the refrigerator overnight, basting frequently with the marinade.

Drain, and place in a roasting pan. Roast in a 350° oven 15 minutes to a pound, or to desired degree of rareness. (In Italy, the lamb is served pink.) Add the marinade after 30 minutes roasting time, and baste frequently thereafter.

Serves 6-8.

ABBACCHIO ai PISELLI

Braised Lamb with Peas

3 pounds boneless lamb, cut in 1½-inch cubes	1 tablespoon flour
3 tablespoons butter	16 small white onions
2 teaspoons salt	¾ cup boiling water
½ teaspoon freshly ground black pepper	½ cup peeled diced tomatoes
	2 pounds green peas or 2 packages frozen

Brown the lamb in the butter; sprinkle with the salt, pepper and flour. Add the onions. Cook 2 minutes. Mix in the water and tomatoes; cover and cook over low heat 1 hour or until tender.

While the lamb is cooking, half-cook the peas. Drain and add to the lamb; cook 5 minutes longer.

Serves 6-8.

ABBACCHIO alla CACCIATORA

Lamb, Hunter's Style

3 pounds boneless spring lamb	3 anchovy fillets
1½ teaspoons salt	2 cloves garlic, minced
½ teaspoon freshly ground black pepper	1 teaspoon rosemary
3 tablespoons olive oil	⅓ cup wine vinegar
	2 tablespoons minced parsley

Have the lamb cut in 2-inch pieces. Toss with the salt and pepper. Heat the oil in a Dutch oven or heavy deep skillet; brown the lamb in it. Cover and cook over low heat 1 hour or until tender. If necessary, add very small amounts of boiling water to keep from burning.

Mash together the anchovies, garlic and rosemary; mix in the vinegar. Stir into the lamb; cook over high heat 5 minutes. Sprinkle with the parsley.

Serves 6-8.

ABBACCHIO SBRODETTATO

Lamb in Egg Sauce

3 pounds boneless lamb, cut in 2-inch cubes	⅓ cup chopped onions
¼ cup flour	1 clove garlic, minced
2 teaspoons salt	⅛ teaspoon crushed dried red pepper
½ teaspoon freshly ground black pepper	1 cup dry white wine
4 tablespoons butter	2 eggs
	2 tablespoons cold water
1 teaspoon grated lemon rind	

Toss the lamb in a mixture of the flour, salt, and pepper. Melt the butter in a Dutch oven or heavy saucepan; sauté the onions 10 minutes. Mix in the garlic, red pepper, and lamb. Cover and cook over low heat 20 minutes or until lamb browns. Shake the pan frequently. Add ¼ cup wine; recover and cook 45 minutes or until lamb is tender, adding ¼ cup wine every 15 minutes.

Beat together the eggs, water, and lemon rind. Add a little of the pan juices, stirring steadily to prevent curdling. Mix into the lamb; cook over very low heat 2 minutes, stirring steadily. Remove from heat and let stand 2 minutes before serving.

Serves 6-8.

ABBACCHIO PASTICCIARE

Lamb Casserole

- 6 loin lamb chops, cut 1-inch thick
- 1½ pounds tomatoes, sliced
- 3 teaspoons salt
- ¾ teaspoon freshly ground black pepper
- ½ teaspoon basil
- 1 medium eggplant, peeled and sliced thin
- 2 green peppers, cut in eighths lengthwise
- 1 cup raw rice
- 1 cup puréed canned tomatoes
- 3 tablespoons olive oil

Brown the chops on both sides in a skillet; drain.

In a casserole, spread half the tomatoes; sprinkle with a little of the salt, pepper, and basil. Make layers of half the eggplant and green peppers, sprinkling each layer with seasoning. Repeat the sequence, then spread rice over all. Arrange chops over it and season. Add the puréed tomatoes and sprinkle with the olive oil. Cover and bake in a 400° oven 1¼ hours, adding very little boiling water if necessary to keep from burning. Remove cover and bake 10 minutes longer.

Serves 6.

COSTATELLE d'AGNELLO

Lamb Chops in White Wine

- 4 shoulder lamb chops, cut 1-inch thick
- 1½ teaspoons salt
- ½ teaspoon freshly ground black pepper
- 2 tablespoons butter
- 1 cup dry white wine
- ½ teaspoon rosemary
- 1 clove garlic, minced
- 1 teaspoon grated lemon rind
- 1 bay leaf

2 tablespoons minced parsley

Trim the fat off the lamb; rub the chops with a mixture of the salt, pepper, and flour. Melt the butter in a heavy skillet; brown the chops in it. Pour off the fat. Add the wine, rosemary, garlic, lemon rind and bay leaf. Bring to a boil, cover and cook over low heat 45 minutes or until tender. Sprinkle with the parsley before serving.

Serves 4.

ARISTA alla FIORENTINA

Roast Pork, Florence Style

8-rib loin of pork	2½ teaspoons salt
3 cloves garlic, cut in slivers	¾ teaspoons freshly ground black pepper
½ teaspoon rosemary	
2 cups water	

Trim the fat off the pork. Make a few incisions in the pork. Dip the garlic in the rosemary and insert it in the cuts. Rub the pork with the salt and pepper. Place in a shallow roasting pan with the water. Roast in a 350° oven 3 hours. After the pork is browned, begin basting it every half hour. Serve cold or hot, but in Florence the meat is customarily served cold.

Serves 4-6.

BRACIOLINE di MAIALE al POMODORO

Pork Chops in Tomato Sauce

6 pork chops, cut ¾-inch thick	½ cup dry red wine
2 teaspoons salt	¼ cup Marsala or sweet sherry
½ teaspoon freshly ground black pepper	¾ cup peeled chopped tomatoes
2 tablespoons olive oil	1 clove garlic, minced
2 tablespoons minced parsley	

Trim the fat from the pork and pound the chops a little to flatten. Season with the salt and pepper.

Heat the oil in a skillet; brown the chops on both sides.

Pour off the fat. Add the wine; cook over medium heat 5 minutes. Add the tomatoes and garlic; cover and cook over low heat 25 minutes, mixing and turning the chops frequently. Sprinkle with the parsley.

Serves 6.

COSTATELLE di MAIALE alla MILANESE

Breaded Pork Chops

- 4 pork chops, cut 1-inch thick
- 1 egg, beaten
- 1½ teaspoons salt
- ¼ teaspoon freshly ground black pepper
- ⅓ cup grated Parmesan cheese
- ⅓ cup dry bread crumbs
- 2 tablespoons olive oil
- 2 tablespoons butter

Trim the fat from the chops. Dip in a mixture of the egg; salt and pepper, then the cheese mixed with the bread crumbs.

Heat the olive oil and butter in a skillet, (with ovenproof handle). Brown the chops on both sides on direct low heat, then bake in a 350° oven 35 minutes or until tender and no pink remains. Turn the chops twice.

Serves 4.

BRACIOLINE di MAIALE alla TOSCANA

Braised Pork Chops

- 6 pork chops, cut ¾-inch thick
- 2 teaspoons salt
- ½ teaspoon freshly ground black pepper
- ⅛ teaspoon fennel seeds
- 2 tablespoons olive oil
- 1 clove garlic, minced
- ½ cup boiling water

Trim the fat from the pork; season with the salt, pepper, and fennel.

Heat the oil in a skillet. Add the chops and garlic.

Brown over high heat. Pour off the fat and add the water. Cover and cook over low heat 30 minutes.

Serves 6.

CASOEULA

Pork Casserole

8 pork chops, cut ¾-inch thick	1 cup thinly sliced carrots
1½ teaspoon salt	1 tablespoon flour
½ teaspoon freshly ground black pepper	½ pound Italian sausages, sliced
3 slices bacon, diced	1½ cups dry white wine
	1 bay leaf
3-pound head cabbage	

Season the pork chops with the salt and pepper. Lightly brown the bacon in a casserole. Pour off half the fat. Add the onions and carrots; sauté 5 minutes. Add the chops; brown lightly on both sides. Sprinkle with the flour and add the sausages, wine, and bay leaf; cover and cook over low heat 1¼ hours.

While the pork is cooking, cut the cabbage in eighths; cook in boiling salted water 5 minutes. Drain very well. Add to the casserole; recover and cook 30 minutes longer. Taste for seasoning.

Serves 6-8.

SCALOPPINE al CARCIOFI

Veal and Artichokes

1 package frozen artichoke hearts, thawed	¼ teaspoon freshly ground pepper
3 tablespoons butter	3 tablespoons olive oil
2½ teaspoons salt	¼ cup beef broth
12 veal scallops	⅓ cup grated Parmesan cheese
1 egg, beaten	
¼ cup flour	

Sauté the artichokes in the butter 5 minutes. Season with 1 teaspoon salt. Dip the scallops in the egg, then in a mixture of the flour, pepper, and remaining salt.

Heat the oil in a skillet; brown the veal on both sides. Arrange in a greased shallow casserole (or use skillet, if it has ovenproof handle). Add the broth, cover veal with artichokes and sprinkle with the cheese. Bake in a 375° oven 10 minutes or until browned.

Serves 6.

VITELLO ARROSTO

Roast Veal

- 4 pounds rolled leg or loin of veal
- 2 slices prosciutto ham
- 2 teaspoons salt
- ½ teaspoon freshly ground black pepper
- ¼ teaspoon marjoram
- ¼ teaspoon thyme
- 3 tablespoons soft butter
- 1 cup sliced onions
- ½ cup grated carrots
- ¼ cup sliced celery
- 1 cup dry white wine
- ¼ cup light cream
- 2 teaspoons flour
- ¾ cups beef broth
- 1 cup chopped mushrooms
- 2 tablespoons minced parsley

Use a sharp knife or larding needle and pierce the veal in several places. Cut the ham in strips and press into the openings. Rub the veal with a mixture of the salt, pepper, marjoram, and thyme; spread with the butter. Place in a roasing pan with the onions, carrots and celery around it.

Roast in a 400° oven 25 minutes. Stir the wine and cream into the pan; baste several times. Reduce the heat to 300° and roast the veal 2 hours longer, basting frequently. Transfer the veal to a heated serving dish and keep warm. Purée the vegetables and gravy in an electric blender or mash smooth.

In a saucepan, combine the flour, broth, mushrooms, and parsley. Bring to a boil, stirring constantly. Add the gravy; cook over low heat 10 minutes. Taste for seasoning. Carve the veal and pour sauce over all.

Serves 6-8.

OSSI BUCHI
Braised Veal Shins

- 3 pounds veal shin
- ¼ cup flour
- 2 tablespoons olive oil
- 2 tablespoons butter
- 2 teaspoons salt
- ½ teaspoon freshly ground black pepper
- ¼ teaspoon rosemary
- ¾ cup chopped onions
- ¼ cup grated carrots
- 1 stalk celery, chopped
- 1 cup dry white wine
- 1 tablespoon tomato paste
- ½ cup water
- 2 tablespoons grated lemon rind
- 1 clove garlic, minced
- 2 tablespoons minced parsley

Have the veal shins sawed into 2-inch pieces—be sure they're meaty. Roll lightly in the flour.

Heat the oil and butter in a Dutch oven or heavy saucepan; brown the shins in it. Sprinkle with the salt, pepper and rosemary. Add the onions, carrots, and celery. Cook 5 minutes. Add the wine, tomato paste and water. Cover and cook over low heat 2 hours, or until tender. Add small amounts of boiling water from time to time if necessary. Mix together the lemon rind, garlic, and parsley; stir into the gravy. Recover and cook 5 minutes longer. Serve with *risotto* or boiled rice.

Serves 6.

LOMBATINA con VERDURE
Veal Chops with Vegetables

- 6 veal chops, cut 1-inch thick
- ¼ cup flour
- 2 teaspoons salt
- ¼ teaspoon freshly ground black pepper
- ½ teaspoon thyme
- 2 tablespoons olive oil
- 4 tablespoons butter
- ½ cup Marsala or sweet sherry
- 2 tablespoons heavy cream
- 1 cup sautéed sliced mushrooms
- 18 cooked asparagus
- 2 cups cooked green peas

Dip the chops in a mixture of the flour, salt, pepper, and thyme. Heat the oil and 2 tablespoons butter in a skillet; brown the chops in it on both sides. Add the wine; cover and cook over low heat 15 minutes or until chops are tender. Stir in the cream.

Arrange the chops on a heated serving dish; spread the mushrooms over them and arrange the asparagus on top. Dot with the remaining butter and surround with the peas.

Serves 6.

LOMATINE al CARTOCCIO
Veal Chops in Paper

- 2 tablespoons butter
- ¼ pound mushrooms, thinly sliced
- 1 cup peeled diced tomatoes
- ¼ cup julienne-cut ham
- ¼ cup dry white wine
- 2½ teaspoons salt
- ½ teaspoon freshly ground black pepper
- 6 veal chops, cut 1-inch thick
- 3 tablespoons olive oil
- 2 tablespoons minced parsley

Melt the butter in a saucepan; sauté the mushrooms 3 minutes. Add the tomatoes, ham, wine, 1 teaspoon salt and ¼ teaspoon pepper. Bring to a boil and cook over low heat 10 minutes.

Season the chops with the remaining salt and pepper. Heat 2 tablespoons oil in a skillet; brown the chops in it on both sides. Cut 6 pieces of parchment paper or aluminum foil large enough to completely enclose the chops. Brush with remaining oil. Place a chop in the center of each and cover with the sauce. Sprinkle with the parsley. Fold over the paper, sealing the edges well. Place on a baking sheet; bake in a 375° oven 15 minutes or until chops are tender. Serve in the paper, with the top rolled back.

Serves 6.

COSTOLETTE di VITELLO con FORMAGGIO

Veal with Cheese

- ½ cup heavy cream
- 3 tablespoons grated Parmesan cheese
- ¼ pound mozzarella cheese, cubed
- ½ cup julienne-cut ham
- 1 egg
- ¼ teaspoon freshly ground black pepper
- 3 tablespoons butter
- 8 veal scallops
- 1 teaspoon salt

In the top of a double boiler combine the cream, cheeses and ham. Place over hot water until cheese melts. Beat the egg and pepper in a bowl; add the cheese mixture, stirring steadily to prevent curdling.

Melt the butter in a skillet; brown the veal on both sides. Season with the salt, then spoon the cheese mixture over them. Place under a hot broiler until browned.

Serves 4.

INVOLTO di VITELLO alla MILANESE

Veal Rolls Milanese

- 14 veal scallops
- 1 clove garlic, minced
- ¼ cup finely chopped parsley
- 2 tablespoons dry white wine
- ¼ teaspoon sage
- ⅛ teaspoon nutmeg
- 2 teaspoons salt
- ½ teaspoon freshly ground black pepper
- ⅓ cup flour
- 6 tablespoons butter

Grind 2 veal scallops in a food chopper. Mix in the garlic, parsley, wine, nutmeg, ¾ teaspoon salt, and ¼ teaspoon pepper. Spread some of the mixture on each of the 12 scallops, roll up and tie with white thread.

Mix the flour with the remaining salt and pepper; dip the rolls in the mixture. Melt the butter in a skillet; add the sage and rolls. Sauté 20 minutes or until browned on all sides and tender.

Serves 6.

VALDOSTANA di VITELLO

Veal and Ham, Milan Style

5 slices prosciutto ham
10 veal scallops
5 tablespoons cream cheese
1 tablespoon minced truffles
2 teaspoons salt
½ teaspoon freshly ground black pepper
Flour
6 tablespoons butter
½ cup dry white wine

Place a slice of prosciutto ham on 5 scallops. Spread each with some cream cheese and sprinkle with the truffles. Cover with the remaining veal and pound the edges together. Season with the salt and pepper; dip in the flour.

Sauté the veal in the butter until browned on both sides. Add the wine; cover and cook over low heat 20 minutes or until tender.

Serves 5.

SCALOPPINE di VITELLA al PROSCIUTTO

Veal with Ham

6 very thin veal cutlets
1¼ teaspoons salt
¼ teaspoon freshly ground black pepper
4 tablespoons butter
6 slices prosciutto or cooked ham
1 cup sliced sautéed mushrooms
1½ cups cooked green peas
¾ cup dry white wine
2 tablespoons minced parsley

Pound the veal very thin; season with the salt and pepper. Melt the butter in a skillet; brown the veal on both sides. Place a slice of ham on each cutlet; add the mushrooms, peas and wine. Cook over low heat 10 minutes. Sprinkle with the parsley.

Serves 6.

SCALOPPINE RIPIENE

Ham-Stuffed Veal Rolls

8 veal scallops (1 pound)	**2 tablespoons grated**
1¼ teaspoons salt	**Parmesan cheese**
¼ teaspoon freshly ground	**1 tablespoon Marsala or**
black pepper	**sweet sherry**
¾ cup finely chopped ham	**¼ cup flour**
¼ cup chopped mushrooms	**4 tablespoons butter**
½ cup dry white wine	

Pound the scallops as thin as possible. Season one side with the salt and pepper. Mix together the ham, mushrooms, cheese, and marsala. Spread 2 heaping tablespoons on the unseasoned side of the veal. Roll up and tie with thread or fasten with tootpicks. Roll in the flour.

Melt the butter in a skillet; brown the rolls in it. Add the wine. Cover over low heat 15 minutes or until tender and wine almost absorbed.

Serves 4.

BRACIOLETTE RIPIENE

Stuffed Veal Rolls

¾ cup minced parsley	**1¼ teaspoons salt**
½ cup blanched sliced	**¼ teaspoon freshly ground**
almonds	**black pepper**
2 tablespoons grated	**12 thin slices cooked ham**
Parmesan cheese	**4 tablespoons butter**
12 veal scallops	**¾ cup dry white wine**

Mix together the parsley, almonds, and cheese. Have the veal pounded very thin. Season 1 side with salt and pepper. On the unseasoned sides, place a slice of ham cut to fit the veal. Put some of the parsley mixture on each, and roll up. Tie with thread or fasten with toothpicks.

Melt the butter in a skillet; brown the rolls on all sides. Add the wine, bring to a boil, cover, and cook over low heat 20 minutes.

Serves 4-6.

SALTIMBOCCA
Veal and Ham Rolls

12 veal scallops	12 slices prosciutto ham
1¼ teaspoons salt	12 fresh sage leaves or
¼ teaspoon freshly ground black pepper	½ teaspoon, dried
	4 tablespoons butter
¾ cup dry white wine	

Have the veal pounded as thin as possible; season with the salt and pepper. Place a slice of ham (cut to same size) over each slice of veal. Put a sage leaf on each, or sprinkle with the dried sage. Roll up, veal side out, and fasten with toothpicks or tie with thread.

Melt the butter in a skillet; brown the rolls in it on all sides. Add the wine; cover and cook over low heat 20 minutes or until the veal is tender. Remove thread or toothpicks.

Serves 6.

ROLE di VITELLO
Rolled Veal and Ham

1½ pounds veal steak, cut ½-inch thick	½ teaspoon freshly ground black pepper
¼ pound prosciutto or cooked ham	2 tablespoons olive oil
	3 tablespoons butter
2 carrots, julienne cut	1 cup dry white wine
1½ teaspoons salt	⅛ teaspoon sage

Have the veal pounded as thin as possible. Arrange the ham over it, then the carrots. Roll up and tie with thread. Rub with the salt and pepper.

Heat the oil and butter in a Dutch oven or heavy saucepan; brown the veal in it on all sides. Add the wine and sage. Cover and cook over low heat 2 hours or until tender. Baste and turn veal a few times. Slice and serve with gravy.

Serves 4-6.

INVOLTINI di VITELLO
Veal Rolls

- 8 veal scallops
- ¾ cup ricotta cheese or ½ cup cottage cheese mixed with ¼ cup cream cheese
- ½ cup finely chopped ham
- ¼ cup flour
- 1½ teaspoons salt
- ¼ teaspoon pepper
- 3 tablespoons olive oil
- 3 tablespoons butter
- 2 tablespoons Marsala or sweet sherry

Have the veal pounded very thin. Mix together the cheese and ham; spread on the veal and roll up. Tie with thread or fasten with toothpicks. Dip in a mixture of the flour, salt, and pepper.

Heat the oil and butter in a skillet; sauté the rolls 30 minutes, turning them frequently. Transfer the rolls to a heated serving dish. Stir the wine into the pan, scraping the bottom of browned particles. Pour over the rolls.

Serves 4.

VITELLO alla PAESANA
Veal, Country Style

- 1 breast of veal
- 2 tablespoons olive oil
- 2 tablespoons butter
- ¾ cup chopped onions
- ¼ cup chopped celery
- 2 cups peeled cubed tomatoes
- 2 teaspoons salt
- ½ teaspoon freshly ground black pepper
- ½ teaspoon basil
- ½ cup hot beef broth
- 1 package frozen peas and carrots, thawed
- 2 tablespoons minced parsley

Meats / 119

Have the veal cut up into serving-sized pieces, bone and all. Heat the oil and butter in a Dutch oven or heavy casserole; sauté the onions and celery 5 minutes. Add the veal; cook until browned. Add the tomatoes, salt, pepper, and basil. Cover and bake in a 300° oven 1¼ hours, adding the broth from time to time. Skim the fat. Add the peas and carrots; recover and bake 15 minutes longer. Sprinkle with the parsley.

Serves 4-5.

PICCATE al MARSALA

Veal Scallops with Marsala

16 veal scallops (1¼ pounds)	4 tablespoons butter
⅓ cup flour	¼ cup Marsala or sweet sherry
2 teaspoons salt	2 tablespoons chicken broth or water
½ teaspoon freshly ground black pepper	

The scallops must be paper thin and cut small. Each scallop should weigh little more than 1 ounce. Dip in a mixture of the flour, salt, and pepper.

Melt the butter in a heavy skillet; brown the scallops in it on both sides. Add the wine and bring to a boil, then add the broth. Stir well; cook over medium heat 2 minutes.

Serves 4-6.

BRACIOLE di VITELLO RIPIENO

Stuffed Veal Chops

4 veal chops, cut ¾-inch thick	¼ cup flour
4 slices prosciutto ham	1½ teaspoons salt
4 thin slices Mozzarella cheese	¼ teaspoon pepper
	1 egg, beaten
	½ cup dry bread crumbs
4 tablespoons butter	

Split the chops, but leave one side connected. Open the chops (like a book) and pound each side as thin as possible. Place a slice of ham and cheese on each. Close the chops (don't let the cheese come too close to the edges), moisten the edges and press together. Dip lightly in the flour mixed with the salt and pepper, the egg, and finally, the bread crumbs.

Melt the butter in a skillet; sauté the chops 10 minutes on each side or until tender and browned. Serve with lemon wedges.

Serves 4.

VITELLO TONNATO

Veal with Tuna Fish Sauce

- 3 pounds rolled leg of veal
- 1 teaspoon salt
- ½ teaspoon freshly ground black pepper
- ½ cup sliced onion
- 1 carrot, sliced
- 3 sprigs parsley
- 1 clove garlic
- 1 clove
- 4 cups boiling water
- 1 7¾-ounce can tuna fish
- 8 anchovy fillets
- ¼ cup lemon juice
- ¾ cup olive oil
- 2 teaspoons capers

Rub the veal with the salt and ¼ teaspoon pepper. Place in a Dutch oven or heavy saucepan and brown it over high heat. Pour off the fat. Add the onion, carrot, parsley, garlic, clove, and boiling water. Cover and cook over low heat 1½ hours or until tender. Drain, dry and cool.

Purée the tuna fish, anchovies, and lemon juice in an electric blender (or mash very smooth). Very gradually beat in the oil, until the consistency of thin mayonnaise. Mix in the capers.

Place the veal in a glass or pottery bowl; pour sauce over it. Marinate in the refrigerator 24 hours before serving. Slice very thin, and serve with the sauce on top.

Serves 8-12 as a first course.

Meats / 121

POLPETTE al POMODORO

Veal Balls in Tomato Sauce

- 4 tablespoons butter
- ½ cup chopped onions
- 1 clove garlic, minced
- 1 29-ounce can Italian-style tomatoes
- 2½ teaspoons salt
- ½ teaspoon freshly ground black pepper
- 1½ pounds ground raw veal
- 2 eggs, beaten
- 1 tablespoon Marsala or sweet sherry
- ½ cup grated Parmesan cheese
- ¼ cup flour
- 2 tablespoons minced parsley

Melt the butter in a saucepan; sauté the onions 10 minutes. Add the garlic, tomatoes, and half the salt and pepper. Bring to a boil and cook over low heat 20 minutes. Prepare the meat balls meanwhile.

Mix together the veal, eggs, wine, cheese, and remaining salt and pepper. Shape into 1-inch balls and roll lightly in the flour. Add to the sauce; cover and cook over low heat 1 hour. Taste for seasoning and sprinkle with the parsley. Serve with rice or noodles.

Serves 6-8.

POLPETTINE di VITELLO

Veal Croquettes

- 1 pound ground veal
- ½ cup finely chopped onions
- ¼ cup minced parsley
- 1 clove garlic, minced
- 3 eggs, beaten
- 1 tablespoon cold water
- 1½ teaspoons salt
- ½ teaspoon freshly ground black pepper
- ⅓ cup flour
- 4 tablespoons butter
- ⅓ cup Marsala or sweet sherry

Mix together the veal, onions, parsley, garlic, eggs, water, salt, and pepper. Shape into 8 thin croquettes. Chill 2 hours.

Dip the croquettes in the flour. Melt the butter in a skillet; brown the croquettes in it. Add the wine; cook over low heat 15 minutes turning them once.

Serves 4.

SFORMATO di VITELLO

Veal and Zucchini Casserole

- 3 zucchini (1½ pounds)
- 2½ teaspoons salt
- 12 veal scallops
- ½ teaspoon freshly ground black pepper
- ¼ teaspoon nutmeg
- ¾ cup grated Parmesan cheese
- 4 tablespoons butter

Scrub the zucchini and slice very thin. Sprinkle with 1½ teaspoons salt and let stand 1 hour. Drain well. Season the veal with ¼ teaspoon pepper and the remaining salt.

In a buttered shallow casserole or deep pie plate, spread ⅓ of the zucchini; sprinkle with a little pepper and nutmeg. Arrange 6 scallops over it; sprinkle with ¼ cup cheese and dot with 1 tablespoon butter. Cover with ⅓ the zucchini, season, arrange remaining veal over it, sprinkle with ¼ cup cheese and dot with 1 tablespoon butter. Cover with remaining zucchini, sprinkle with the remaining cheese and dot with remaining butter.

Bake in a 350° oven 45 minutes.

Serves 4-6.

SPEZZATINO di VITELLO

Veal Stew

- 3 pounds shoulder or leg of veal
- 3 tablespoons butter
- 2 tablespoons olive oil
- 1 cup thinly sliced onions
- 2 teaspoons salt
- ½ teaspoon freshly ground black pepper
- ¾ cup dry white wine
- 1½ cups peeled diced tomatoes
- 3 green peppers, cut in strips
- 1 pound green peas, shelled or 1 package frozen, thawed

Cut the veal in 2-inch cubes. Heat the butter and oil in a Dutch oven or heavy saucepan. Sauté the onions 10 minutes. Add the veal; cook until browned. Season with the salt and pepper; add the wine. Cook over medium heat 5 minutes. Add the tomatoes and green peppers; cover and cook over low heat 2 hours. Fifteen minutes before the end of the cooking time add the fresh peas, (or 10 minutes, if frozen are used).

Serves 6-8.

SCALOPPINE al FEGATO
Veal with Chicken Livers

- 8 veal scallops (1 pound)
- ¼ cup flour
- 2½ teaspoons salt
- ¾ teaspoon freshly ground black pepper
- ¼ cup olive oil
- ½ pound chicken livers, diced
- ½ cup peeled chopped tomatoes
- ¼ teaspoon thyme

Have the veal pounded as thin as possible; dip in a mixture of the flour and half the salt and pepper.

Heat the oil in a skillet; brown 1 minute on each side over high heat. Add the livers; cook over high heat 3 minutes. Add the tomatoes, thyme, and the remaining salt and pepper; cook over medium heat 5 minutes longer. Serve with *risotto* (see recipe).

Serves 4-5.

ANIMELLE alla CIOCIARA
Sweetbreads, Ham and Mushrooms

- 3 pair sweetbreads
- 1 tablespoon vinegar
- 2 teaspoons salt
- ¼ cup flour
- 4 tablespoons olive oil
- 4 tablespoons butter
- ¼ teaspoon white pepper
- 1 cup sliced sautéed mushrooms
- ½ cup julienne cut prosciutto or cooked ham
- ¾ cup peeled diced tomatoes
- ¾ cup dry white wine

Wash the sweetbreads, cover with cold water and let soak 1 hour. Drain, add fresh water to cover, the vinegar and 1 teaspoon salt. Bring to a boil and cook over low heat 5 minutes. Drain, cover with cold water and let stand 20 minutes. Drain, remove the membranes and tubes, but leave each half whole. Dry, then dip lightly in the flour.

Heat the oil in a skillet; brown the sweetbreads in it. Pour off the oil. Add the butter, pepper, mushrooms, ham, tomatoes, wine and the remaining salt. Bring to a boil and cook over low heat 10 minutes.

Serves 6.

CROCCHETTE di CERVELLA

Brain Croquettes

1 pound calf's brains	½ cup sautéed chopped onions
1 tablespoon vinegar	
1¼ teaspoons salt	1 egg, beaten
¼ teaspoon white pepper	¼ cup flour
4 tablespoons butter	

Wash the brains, cover with cold water and let stand 10 minutes. Drain, add fresh water to cover and the vinegar. Bring to a boil and cook over low heat 15 minutes. Drain and cover with cold water; let stand 15 minutes. Drain, remove the membranes and mash the brains to a paste. Mix in the salt, pepper, and onions. Chill. Form into 8 croquettes; dip in the egg, then in the flour.

Melt the butter in a skillet; brown the croquettes on both sides. Serve with lemon wedges.

Serves 4.

FEGATO di VITELLO al MARSALA

Calf's Liver in Marsala

1 pound calf's liver, cut ⅛-inch thick	1⅓ teaspoon salt
	4 tablespoons butter
2 tablespoons lemon juice	3 tablespoons Marsala or sweet sherry
¼ teaspoon white pepper	
⅓ cup flour	

Wash and dry the liver; rub with the lemon juice and pepper, then dip in the flour mixed with the salt. Melt the butter in a skillet; fry the liver over high heat 1 minute on each side. Stir the wine into the pan; cook over low heat 2 minutes, basting almost constantly.

Serves 4.

FEGATO di VITELLO alla MILANESE

Breaded Calf's Liver

1 pound calf's liver, cut ¼-inch thick	1 egg
2 tablespoons lemon juice	1 tablespoon water
½ teaspoon freshly ground black pepper	½ cup dry bread crumbs
	1¼ teaspoons salt
	4 tablespoons butter
2 tablespoons minced parsley	

Wash and dry the liver; rub with the lemon juice and pepper. Let stand in the refrigerator 1 hour.

Beat the egg and water together; dip the liver slices in it and then in the bread crumbs mixed with the salt. Melt the butter in a skillet; sauté the liver 3 minutes on each side or to desired degree of rareness. Stir the parsley into the butter.

Serves 4.

RIGNONI TRIFOLATI

Braised Kidneys

1 pound veal kidneys	1 teaspoon grated lemon rind
3 cups boiling water	
2 tablespoons lemon juice	½ cup Marsala or sweet sherry
4 tablespoons butter	
1¼ teaspoons salt	3 tablespoons minced parsley
¼ teaspoon freshly ground black pepper	

Wash the kidneys, cut in half and remove the core. Soak

in the boiling water mixed with the lemon juice for 3 minutes. Drain, then slice thin.

Melt the butter in a skillet; sauté the kidneys 5 minutes. Season with the salt, pepper and lemon rind and add the wine. Cook over medium heat 5 minutes. Sprinkle with the parsley.

Serves 4.

ROGNONI al VINO BIANCO

Kidneys in White Wine

1 pound veal kidneys	4 tablespoons butter
Boiling water	2 cups thinly sliced onions
½ cup warm dry white wine	1½ teaspoons salt
¼ teaspoon freshly ground black pepper	

Wash the kidneys, cut in half and remove the core. Soak in boiling water 5 minutes. Drain, dry and slice. Marinate in the wine 1 hour. Drain and dry, reserving the marinade.

While the kidneys are marinating, prepare the onions. Melt the butter in a skillet; sauté the onions over very low heat until soft and yellow. Add the kidneys, the salt, pepper, and ¼ cup of the reserved wine; cover and cook over low heat 15 minutes, adding the remaining wine after 10 minutes. Serve with sautéed Italian or French bread.

Serves 4.

TRIPPA alla FIORENTINA

Tripe in Meat Sauce

2 pounds tripe	¼ cup water
2 tablespoons butter	2 teaspoons salt
¾ cup chopped onions	½ teaspoon freshly ground black pepper
¼ cup grated carrots	½ teaspoon marjoram
½ pound beef	½ cup grated Parmesan cheese
½ cup dry white wine	
¾ cup peeled chopped tomatoes	

Wash the tripe, cover with water and bring to a boil; cook over low heat 1 hour. Drain, cool and cut into 2-inch long by ½-inch wide strips. Prepare the sauce while the tripe is cooking.

Melt the butter in a saucepan; brown the onions, carrots, and beef in it. Add the wine, tomatoes, water, salt, and pepper; bring to a boil, cover and cook over low heat 1 hour. Add the marjoram and tripe; recover and cook 1 hour longer. Remove the beef and sprinkle with cheese.

Serves 6-8.

FRITTO MISTO

Mixed Fried Foods

Ingredients used in a Fritto Misto vary from region to region. In Northern Italy, a variety of the following is customary: parboiled sweetbreads and brains, chicken or calf's liver, breast of chicken, scallopine of veal, sliced eggplant, sliced zucchini, sliced artichokes, mushrooms, cauliflower flowerets, green beans. Cut in bite-sized pieces and sprinkle with salt and pepper before digging in the batter.

Batter:

2 cups sifted flour	⅓ cup oil
¾ teaspoon salt	1½ cups lukewarm water
¼ teaspoon white pepper	3 egg whites, beaten stiff
Vegetable oil for deep frying	

Sift the flour, salt, and pepper into a bowl. Mix in the oil, then gradually beat in the water until it is the consistency of heavy cream. Let stand 2 hours. When ready to use, fold in the egg whites. Dip the selected ingredients in the batter.

Heat the oil to 370°. Fry a few pieces at a time until browned. Drain and keep warm while preparing the balance. Serve sprinkled with parsley and surrounded with lemon wedges.

Makes enough batter to serve 6-8.

BOLLITO MISTO
Boiled Mixed Meats

A variety of meats are used in the traditional Bollito Misto. It is best to prepare this dish for at least 8 people, so that enough different meats can be included. However, at least 2 different meats and a sausage should be used. Here are some suggestions:

A small smoked tongue
2 whole onions
2 carrots
2 stalks celery
4 sprigs parsley
An eye round of beef

A piece of rolled veal
A small fowl
Italian pork sausages
½ teaspoon freshly ground black pepper

Cover the tongue with water, bring to a boil and drain. Add fresh boiling water to cover, the onions, carrots, celery, and parsley. Bring to a boil and cook over low heat 1 hour. Skim the top. Add the beef and veal, cook 1 hour. Skim the top. Add the chicken, sausages and pepper. Cook 1 hour. Taste for seasoning, adding salt if necessary. Arrange the meats on a serving dish and serve with mustard, tomato sauce, and/or béarnaise sauce. Strain the broth and use for other purposes.

Chapter 9

Vegetables

CARCIOFI alla ROMANA
Roman-Style Artichokes

6 small artichokes	2 teaspoons salt
4 cloves garlic, minced	½ teaspoon freshly ground black pepper
1 cup minced parsley	
1 teaspoon fresh mint, chopped or ⅛ teaspoon dried	¼ cup olive oil
	1 cup dry white wine
	½ cup chicken broth

Buy very young artichokes. Remove the tough outer leaves and cut off the points of the others. Carefully force the centers apart and cut out the chokes. Stuff the centers with a mixture of the garlic, parsley, mint, 1 teaspoon salt and ¼ teaspoon pepper. Arrange close together in a casserole; sprinkle with the oil. Cook over medium heat 10 minutes. Add the wine, broth, and remaining salt and pepper. Cover and cook over medium heat 45 minutes or until artichokes are tender.

Serves 6.

ASPARAGI PARMIGIANA
Asparagus (with) Parmesan Cheese

3 packages frozen asparagus tips	½ cup grated Parmesan cheese
½ cup melted butter	

Cook the asparagus 2 minutes less than package directs. Drain well. Arrange in a single layer in a buttered shallow baking dish. Pour the butter over them and sprinkle with the cheese. Bake in a preheated 400° oven 10 minutes or until lightly browned.

Serves 6-8.

FAGIOLINI al PROSCIUTTO

Green Beans with Ham

2 pounds green beans or 2 packages frozen	¼ teaspoon freshly ground black pepper
4 tablespoons butter	2 tablespoons minced parsley
¼ pound prosciutto or cooked ham, cut julienne	⅛ teaspoon minced garlic

Cook the beans in boiling salted water until tender but firm. Drain.

Melt the butter in a skillet; sauté the ham 3 minutes. Mix in the beans, pepper and salt to taste. Sauté 2 minutes, mixing lightly constantly. Stir in the parsley and garlic.

Serves 6-8.

FAGIOLINI all'ITALIANA

Italian-Style Green Beans

3 tablespoons olive oil	¼ teaspoon pepper
1 cup chopped onions	½ teaspoon oregano
1 clove garlic, minced	1 bay leaf
1 29-ounce can Italian-style tomatoes	2 pounds green beans, cut in half or 2 packages frozen
1½ teaspoons salt	

Heat the oil in a saucepan; sauté the onions and garlic 5 minutes. Add the tomatoes, salt, pepper, oregano, and bay leaf. Bring to a boil and cook over low heat 30 minutes. Add the beans; cover and cook over low heat 45 minutes.

Serves 4-6.

FAGIOLI en SALSA

Italian-Style Green Beans

3 tablespoons olive oil
1 cup chopped onions
1 clove garlic, minced
1 29-ounce can tomatoes
1½ teaspoons salt
¼ teaspoon pepper
½ teaspoon oregano
1 bay leaf
2 pounds green beans, cut in half, or 2 packages frozen

Heat the oil in a saucean; sauté the onions and garlic 5 minutes. Add the tomatoes, salt, pepper, oregano, and bay leaf. Bring to a boil and cook over low heat 30 minutes. Add the beans; cover and cook over low heat 45 minutes.

Serves 4-6.

FAGIOLI alla TOSCANA

Tuscan Style Beans

1½ cups dried white beans
2½ teaspoons salt
¾ cup olive oil
2 cups thinly sliced onions
½ teaspoon freshly ground black pepper
2 tablespoons minced parsley

Wash the beans, removing any imperfect ones. Cover with water, bring to a boil and let soak 1 hour. Drain. Add fresh water to cover and bring to a boil. Cover and cook over low heat 45 minutes. Add half the salt, recover and cook 45 minutes longer or until tender. Drain.

Heat the oil in a skillet; sauté the onions until yellow and transparent. Add to the beans with the pepper and remaining salt; toss lightly. Chill. Sprinkle with the parsley. Serve as an hors d'oeuvre.

Serves 6-8.

FAVE FRESCHE STUFATO

Lima Beans with Ham

- 3 tablespoons butter
- ½ cup finely chopped onions
- ½ cup julienne-cut prosciutto or cooked ham
- 1 cup shredded lettuce
- 2 packages frozen lima beans, thawed
- 1 teaspoon salt
- ¼ teaspoon freshly ground black pepper
- ¾ cup boiling water

Melt the butter in a skillet; sauté the onions 5 minutes. Mix in the ham for 1 minute. Add the lettuce, beans, salt, pepper, and water. Bring to a boil, cover, and cook over low heat 10 minutes or until tender and liquid absorbed.

Serves 6-8.

FASOEIL al FORNO

Baked Red Beans

- 2 cups dried red beans
- 1 cup minced parsley
- 2 cloves garlic, minced
- ½ teaspoon freshly ground black pepper
- ¼ teaspoon mace
- ⅛ ground cloves
- 4 slices salt pork
- 2 teaspoons salt

Wash the beans, cover with water, and bring to a boil. Let soak 1 hour. Drain.

In an earthenware bean pot, sprinkle the parsley, garlic, pepper, mace, and cloves. Cover with the salt pork. Add the beans; very slowly pour in enough water to cover the beans. Cover the pot; bake in 275° oven 5 hours, adding the salt after 3 hours. (If you're in a hurry, bake in a 350° oven 3 hours, and use boiling water.)

Serves 6-8.

CAROTE AGRODOLCE

Sweet and Sour Carrots

10 carrots	3 tablespoons butter
1½ cups water	2 teaspoons flour
1¼ teaspoons salt	2 tablespoons sugar
3 tablespoons cider vinegar	

Wash, scrape, and slice carrots very thin. Bring the water and salt to a boil in a skillet; add the carrots, cover and cook over low heat 5 minutes. Drain, reserving the liquid.

Melt the butter in a saucepan; blend in the flour, then gradually the liquid, stirring steadily to the boiling point. Mix in the sugar and vinegar, then the carrots. Cook over low heat 5 minutes. Taste for seasoning.

Serves 4-6.

CAVOLFIORE alla MILANESE

Cauliflower with Cheese

1 medium-sized cauliflower or 2 packages frozen	2 tablespoons grated Parmesan cheese
½ cup grated Swiss cheese	¼ cup melted butter
2 tablespoons dry bread crumbs	

Remove the leaves of the fresh cauliflower and wash thoroughly. Cook in boiling salted water 15 minutes or until tender but firm. Drain. Cook the frozen cauliflower 2 minutes less than package directs. Drain.

Place the cauliflower in a baking dish. Mix together the Swiss cheese, Parmesan cheese, butter, and bread crumbs; spread over the cauliflower. Bake in a 425° oven 5 minutes or until browned.

Serves 4-6.

SEDANO PARMIGIANA

Celery Parmigiana

3 bunches celery
3 tablespoons butter
½ cup beef broth
1 teaspoon salt
¼ teaspoon freshly ground black pepper
¼ cup chopped ham
¼ cup grated Swiss cheese
¼ cup grated Parmesan cheese

Wash the celery and discard the leaves. Cut each bunch in eighths, lengthwise. Melt the butter in a skillet; sauté the celery 5 minutes, shaking the pan frequently. Add the broth, salt, pepper, and ham. Cover and cook over low heat 15 minutes, shaking the pan frequently. Drain if any liquid remains.

Turn into a buttered baking dish, sprinkle with the mixed cheeses. Bake in a 425° oven 10 minutes or until browned.

Serves 6-8.

MELENZANA alla PARMIGIANA

Baked Eggplant and Cheese

1 medium eggplant
3 teaspoons salt
½ cup flour
¼ cup olive oil
1½ pounds tomatoes, peeled and sliced
½ teaspoon freshly ground black pepper
½ pound mozzarella cheese, thinly sliced
½ cup grated Parmesan cheese
2 tablespoons butter

Peel the eggplant and slice ½-inch thick. Sprinkle with 2 teaspoons salt; let stand 1 hour. Drain and dry thoroughly. Dip in the flour.

Heat 2 tablespoons oil in a skillet; brown the eggplant in it. Put half the slices in a baking dish. Cover with half the tomatoes, sprinkled with pepper and remaining salt, slices of cheese and grated cheese. Repeat the sequence of layers. Dot with butter and sprinkle with the remaining oil. Bake in a 350° oven 25 minutes.

Serves 4-6.

MELENZANA RIPIENE

Stuffed Eggplant

2 medium eggplants	½ teaspoon freshly ground black pepper
6 tablespoons olive oil	
½ cup chopped onions	3 tablespoons dry bread crumbs
½ cup peeled chopped tomatoes	
1¼ teaspoons salt	3 tablespoons grated Parmesan cheese
¼ teaspoon oregano	

Wash and dry the eggplant; remove the stems. Cut in half lengthwise; scoop out the pulp and chop. Reserve shells.

Heat 2 tablespoons oil in a skillet; sauté the onions 5 minutes. Add the eggplant pulp, sauté 5 minutes. Add the tomatoes, salt and pepper; cook 10 minutes. Mix in the bread crumbs, cheese, oregano, and 2 tablespoons oil. Taste for seasoning.

Stuff the shells. Place in a covered baking dish or casserole. Sprinkle with the remaining oil. Cover, and bake in a 375° oven 50 minutes, removing the cover for the last 10 minutes. Serve hot or cold.

Serves 4.

PISELLI alla FIORENTINA

Peas, Florence Style

¼ cup olive oil	½ cup water
1 pound peas, shelled or 1 package, frozen, thawed	2 tablespoons minced parsley
1 clove garlic	1 teaspoon salt
½ cup diced ham	¼ teaspoon white pepper

Combine all the ingredients in a saucepan. Bring to a boil and cook over low heat 15 minutes. Taste for seasoning.

Serves 3-4.

PEPERONI alla ROMANA

Green Peppers, Roman Style

- 4 tablespoons olive oil
- 2 cup coarsely chopped onions
- 4 cups coarsely chopped green peppers
- 1 cup dry white wine
- 1½ teaspoons salt
- ¼ teaspoon freshly ground black pepper
- 2 tablespoons minced parsley

Heat the oil in a skillet; sauté the onions 10 minutes. Add the peppers, wine, salt, and pepper. Cook over low heat 25 minutes or until peppers are tender. Sprinkle with the parsley.

Serves 4-6.

PEPERONI RIPIENO

Stuffed Peppers

- 2 slices white bread, trimmed
- ½ cup milk
- 6 green peppers
- 1 7¾-ounce can tuna fish
- ½ teaspoon salt
- ½ teaspoon freshly ground black pepper
- ½ cup peeled chopped tomatoes
- ¾ cup sliced black olives
- ¼ cup olive oil

Soak the bread in the milk 10 minutes. Drain and mash smooth. Cut 1-inch piece off the stem end of the peppers; scoop out the seeds and fibres.

Drain and flake the tuna fish; mix in the bread, salt, pepper, tomatoes, and olives. Taste for seasoning. Stuff the peppers and arrange in an oiled baking dish. Sprinkle peppers with oil. Cover dish; bake in a 350° oven 50 minutes or until peppers are tender. Serve hot or cold.

Serves 6.

TORTA di PATATA e PROSCIUTTO

Potato Ham Pie

- 1½ pounds potatoes
- 2 teaspoons salt
- ¼ teaspoon white pepper
- ⅛ teaspoon nutmeg
- 6 tablespoons butter
- ¼ cup dry bread crumbs
- ¼ pound Bel Paese or Swiss cheese, cut julienne
- ½ pound prosciutto or cooked ham, cut julienne
- 4 hard-cooked eggs, quartered

Cook the unpeeled potatoes until tender. Drain, peel, and mash smooth with the salt, pepper, nutmeg and 2 tablespoons butter.

Spread 2 tablespoons butter in a 9-inch pie plate. Dust with half the bread crumbs, then cover with half the potatoes. Arrange the cheese, ham and eggs over it, then cover with the remaining potatoes. Sprinkle with the remaining bread crumbs and dot with the remaining butter. Bake in a preheated 400° oven 25 minutes or until browned. Cut into wedges.

Serves 4-6 as a luncheon dish.

CROCCHETTE di PATATE

Potato-Cheese Croquettes

- 2 pounds potatoes
- 4 tablespoons butter
- 3 eggs
- 1 egg yolk
- ½ cup grated Parmesan cheese
- 1¼ teaspoons salt
- ½ teaspoon white pepper
- ¼ teaspoon nutmeg
- ½ cup dry bread crumbs
- 2 cups vegetable oil

Cook the unpeeled potatoes until tender. Drain, peel,

and mash very smooth or put through a ricer. Beat in the butter, 1 egg, the egg yolk, cheese, salt, pepper, and nutmeg. Chill.

Form into 10-12 croquettes. Beat the remaining eggs. Dip the croquettes in them, then in the bread crumbs. Heat the oil in a skillet until it bubbles. Fry the croquettes until browned.

Serves 4-6.

POMODORI GRATINATI

Baked Tomatoes

4 large firm tomatoes	1 clove garlic, minced
1/3 cup dry bread crumbs	1¼ teaspoons salt
3 tablespoons finely chopped parsley	¼ teaspoon freshly ground black pepper
¼ cup olive oil	

Buy even-sized tomatoes. Cut in half crosswise. Mix together the bread crumbs, parsley, garlic, salt, pepper and 2 tablespoons oil. Spread on the cut side of the tomatoes. Arrange in an oiled shallow baking pan; sprinkle with the remaining oil. Bake in a 400° oven 15 minutes or until tomatoes are tender.

Serves 4-8.

POMODORI RIPIENI

Rice-Stuffed Tomatoes

6 large firm tomatoes	1/3 cup boiling water
½ cup olive oil	2 teaspoons salt
½ cup chopped onions	¼ teaspoon freshly ground black pepper
1 cup raw rice	
¼ teaspoon basil	

Buy even-sized tomatoes. Cut a 1-inch piece off the stem end of the tomatoes. Scoop out the pulp and reserve.

Heat 2 tablespoons oil in a skillet; sauté the onions 5 minutes. Mix in the rice until translucent. Add the tomato pulp, water, salt, pepper, and basil. Cook over low heat 10 minutes. Cool and stir in ¼ cup oil. Stuff the tomatoes; arrange in an oiled baking dish; sprinkle with the remaining oil. Cover and bake in a 350° oven 45 minutes, removing the cover for the last 10 minutes. Serve hot or cold.

Serves 6.

ZUCCHINI RIPIENE

Stuffed Zucchini

3 medium zucchini	2 teaspoons salt
⅓ cup olive oil	⅓ teaspoon freshly ground pepper
½ cup minced onions	
1 pound ground beef	¼ teaspoon oregano
½ cup canned tomato sauce	

Buy straight, plump zucchini. Wash, dry, and remove the stems. Cut in half lengthwise. Scoop out the pulp and chop it. Reserve the shells.

Heat 2 tablespoons oil in a skillet; sauté the onions 5 minutes. Mix in the zucchini pulp; sauté 5 minutes. Add the beef; cook until no pink remains, stirring frequently to prevent lumps from forming. Mix in the salt, pepper, and oregano. Stuff the shells. Arrange in an oiled baking dish. Sprinkle with the oil and cover with tomato sauce. Bake in a 350° oven 40 minutes. Taste sauce for seasoning.

Serves 6.

ZUCCHINI GENOVESE

Sautéed Zucchini

1½ pounds small zucchini	2 tablespoons minced
4 tablespoons olive oil	parsley
1 teaspoon salt	1 clove garlic, minced
¼ teaspoon freshly ground black pepper	¼ teaspoon oregano

Wash, scrub, and cut off the stem ends of the zucchini. Cut in pencil thin, 3-inch lengths.

Heat the oil in a skillet; cook the zucchini over high heat until browned, shaking the pan frequently. Add the salt, pepper, parsley, garlic, and oregano. Cook over low heat 5 minutes.

Serves 4-6.

ZUCCHINI in SALSA VERDE

Zucchini in Green Sauce

1½ pounds small zucchini	⅓ cup olive oil
⅓ cup flour	¼ cup minced parsley
1½ teaspoons salt	3 tablespoons wine vinegar
Vegetable oil for deep frying	2 anchovies, minced
	1 clove garlic, minced
½ teaspoon freshly ground black pepper	

Wash, scrub, and thinly slice the zucchini. Toss in a mixture of the flour and salt. Heat the vegetable oil to 380°. Fry the zucchini until browned. Drain well.

Mix together the oil, parsley, vinegar, anchovies, garlic, and pepper. Pour over the zucchini and let marinate 2 hours, turning the mixture occasionally. Serve at room temperature.

Serves 4-6.

Chapter 10

Salads

INSALATA VERDE

Green Salad

A salad is an integral part of an Italian meal. Use crisp greens—escarole, curly endive, thinly sliced fennel, romaine lettuce, etc. Have them washed and thoroughly dried. The dressing consists of 3 parts olive oil, 1 part wine vinegar, salt, freshly ground black pepper, and a little minced garlic, if you like. Toss the dressing with the greens seconds before serving.

INSALATA di RISO

Rice and Vegetable Salad

1 cup rice	1 cup peeled diced tomatoes
1½ cups boiling water	½ cup sliced black olives
2 teaspoons salt	¼ cup chopped anchovies
1 cup julienne-cut celery root	¼ cup olive oil
1 cup sliced bottled artichoke hearts in oil	½ teaspoon freshly ground black pepper
1 cup sliced sautéed mushrooms	½ teaspoon capers
1 7¾-ounce can tuna fish, drained and flaked	1 red onion, thinly sliced

Cook the rice in the boiling water and 1 teaspoon salt in a covered saucepan 15 minutes, or until tender but firm and dry. Cool and toss with a fork to keep grains separate. Add the celery root, artichokes, mushrooms, tuna fish, tomatoes, olives, and anchovies. Toss together with 2 forks, then toss with the oil, pepper, capers, and remaining salt. Heap on a serving dish and arrange onion slices on top.

Serves 4-6.

INSALATA di CIPOLLA

Italian Onion Salad

4 large red Italian or sweet Spanish onions	3 tablespoons wine vinegar
2 teaspoons salt	8 anchovy fillets
½ cup olive oil	¼ cup pitted black olives (Italian or Greek)

Peel the onions and slice paper thin. Cover with ice water; add the salt and a few ice cubes. Let stand 30 minutes. Drain and dry the onions. Put the onions in a salad bowl; sprinkle with a mixture of the oil and vinegar. Arrange the anchovies and olives on top.

Serves 6-8.

Chapter 11

Desserts

BISCUIT TORTONI

1½ cups heavy cream
½ cup sifted confectioners' sugar
3 tablespoons rum or cognac
1 egg white, stiffly beaten
½ cup chopped toasted almonds

Whip the cream until it begins to thicken, then gradually beat in the sugar until stiff. Stir in the rum or cognac. Fold in the egg white.

Spoon into eight to ten 2-3 inch paper cups; sprinkle with the almonds. Freeze 4 hours or until firm.

Serves 8-10.

GELATO di CAFFE

Coffee Ice Cream

8 egg yolks
2½ cups heavy cream
1 tablespoon instant coffee
¾ cup fine granulated sugar

Beat the egg yolks in the top of a double boiler. Stir in the cream and coffee. Place over hot water and cook, stirring steadily until thickened, but do not let broil. Remove from the heat, stir in the sugar for 1 minute, cool, then strain. Turn into 2 dry refrigerator trays. Freeze in the freezer, or refrigerator (control set at coldest point), until edges set. Turn into a bowl and beat with a rotary beater. Return to trays, cover with foil, and freeze until set.

Serves 8-10.

GELATO di FRAGOLE

Strawberry Ice Cream

1 cup sugar	¾ cup water
¼ cup orange juice	2 quarts strawberries
1 tablespoon lemon juice	1 cup heavy cream

Cook the sugar, orange juice, lemon juice and water, stirring steadily to the boiling point; then cook 5 minutes longer, or until syrupy. Cool.

Purée the berries in an electric blender, or force through a sieve. When the syrup is cool, mix it with the berries. Whip the cream and fold it in. Turn into 2 dry ice trays or into a mold. Cover. Put in the freezer for 4 or 5 hours or until firm.

Serves 6-8.

CERTOSINA

Spice-Nut Cake

1 cup sifted flour	½ cup honey
¼ teaspoon salt	⅔ cup water
½ teaspoon baking soda	2½ cups blanched toasted sliced almonds
½ teaspoon ground cloves	
½ teaspoon nutmeg	½ cup finely diced candied fruits
½ teaspoon cinnamon	
½ cup sugar	

Sift together the flour, salt, baking soda, cloves, nutmeg, and cinnamon.

Combine the sugar, honey, and water in a saucepan. Cook over low heat, stirring constantly, until mixture boils. Remove from the heat and beat in the flour mixture until very smooth. Mix in the almonds and fruit. Turn into a well oiled 9-inch pie plate. If you like, decorate the top with almonds and fruit. Bake in a preheated 300° oven 45 minutes or until a cake tester comes out clean. Cool thoroughly before turning out. Serve in very narrow strips.

PANE di SPUGNA

Sponge Cake

1¼ cups sifted flour
¼ teaspoon salt
¼ teaspoon ground anise
8 egg yolks
2 tablespoons cold water
1¼ cups fine granulated sugar
2 tablespoons grated orange rind
8 egg whites

Sift together 3 times the flour, salt, and anise.

Beat the egg yolks and water; gradually beat in ¾ cup sugar until light and fluffy. Fold in the flour mixture and orange rind.

Beat the egg whites until soft peaks form; gradually beat in the remaining sugar until stiff but not dry. Fold into the flour mixture. Turn into an ungreased 9-inch tube pan. Bake in a preheated 350° oven 50 minutes or until browned and shrunk away from side of pan. Invert on a cake rack and let cool in the pan. Run a spatula around the sides and center tube and turn cake out.

AMARETTI

Macaroons

2 egg whites
¼ teaspoon salt
1 cup sugar
1 cup ground blanched almonds
1 teaspoon almond extract

Beat the egg whites and salt until frothy. Gradually beat in the sugar until stiff but not dry. Fold in the almonds and almond extract.

Rinse a cooky sheet with cold water but do not dry it. Drop the mixture onto it by the teaspoon, leaving 1-inch between each. Bake in a preheated 325° oven 20 minutes or until delicately browned and dry. Remove with a spatula.

Makes about 2½ dozen.

CENCI

Fried Crisps

2 cups flour	2 tablespoons sugar
¼ teaspoon salt	1 tablespoon vegetable oil
2 teaspoons baking powder	1 teaspoon almond extract
3 eggs	Fat for deep frying
Confectioners' sugar	

Sift together the flour, salt, and baking powder. Beat the eggs, sugar, oil, and almond extract until thick. Beat in the flour mixture, then turn out onto a floured surface. Knead until smooth. (If too soft, add a little more flour.) Cover with a bowl and let stand 1 hour.

Divide the dough into 2 pieces. Roll out each piece paper thin. Use a fluted pastry wheel or very sharp knife and cut into ¾-inch wide strips 5 inches long. Let stand 10 minutes. Heat the fat to 370°. Fry a few pieces at a time until puffed and browned, about 2 minutes. Drain well and sprinkle with confectioners' sugar.

Makes about 3 dozen.

SFINGE

Crullers

2 cups sifted flour	½ cup sugar
¼ teaspoon salt	1 tablespoon vegetable oil
3 teaspoons baking powder	⅓ cup milk
½ teaspoon mace	Fat for deep frying
2 eggs	Powdered sugar

Sift together the flour, salt, baking powder, and mace. Beat the eggs, sugar, and oil until thick. Stir in the milk, then the flour mixture. Beat until very smooth. Cover with a towel and let stand 15 minutes.

Heat the fat to 370°. Drop the batter into it by the tablespoon, a few at a time. Fry until browned, about 4 minutes. Remove with a slotted spoon and drain. Sprinkle with sugar, anise-flavored if you like.

Makes about 3 dozen.

MONTE BIANCO

Chestnut Dessert

1½ pounds chestnuts	1 cup powdered sugar
3 cups milk	1 cup heavy cream
2 tablespoons cognac	

Cut a crisscross on the pointed end of the chestnuts. Cover with water, bring to a boil, and cook over medium heat 15 minutes. Drain, peel, and remove the inner skin.

Combine the chestnuts and milk; cook over low heat 45 minutes or until very soft. Drain, mash smooth, and beat in the sugar.

Force the chestnut mixture through a ricer or food mill onto a serving dish into a cone-shaped mound. Chill 1 hour. Whip the cream; fold the cognac into it. Completely cover the mound.

Serves 6-8.

PLOMBIERES di CASTAGNE

Frozen Chestnut Dessert

4 eggs	1½ cups canned crème de
⅓ cup sugar	marrons (chestnut
2 cups milk, scalded	purée)
	2 tablespoons cognac
1 cup heavy cream	

In the top of a double boiler, beat the eggs and sugar.

Add the hot milk gradually, stirring steadily to prevent curdling. Place over hot, not boiling water, and cook, stirring constantly until thickened. Remove from the heat; beat in the marrons and cognac. Chill for 3 hours.

Whip the cream and fold into the chestnut mixture. Heap on a serving dish and freeze for 2 hours.

Serves 6-8.

GATO di CASTAGNE
Chestnut Refrigerator Tart

1 pound chestnuts	1 square (ounce) unsweetened chocolate
2 eggs	
½ cup sugar	3 tablespoons cognac
2 cups milk	1 teaspoon vanilla extract
1 cup heavy cream	

Cut a crisscross in the pointed end of the chestnuts. Cover with water, bring to a boil and cook over low heat 40 minutes. Drain, cool slightly, peel and remove inner skin. Purée in an electric blender or force through a sieve. Beat the eggs and sugar in the top of a double boiler. Stir in the milk and the chocolate, broken into small pieces. Place over hot water and cook, stirring constantly until thickened. Beat in the chestnuts, 1 tablespoon cognac, and the vanilla. Cool slightly, then turn into a well greased 7-inch tube pan. Chill 4 hours or until firm. Carefully unmold onto a serving dish. Fill center with the cream, whipped, and flavored with remaining cognac.

Serves 6-8.

PESCHE RIPIENE
Stuffed Baked Peaches

6 large firm peaches	1 egg yolk, beaten
2 tablespoons butter	1 tablespoon cognac
1½ tablespoons sugar	4 tablespoons Marsala or sweet sherry
¾ cup macaroon crumbs	
¼ cup water	

Peel the peaches, cut in half, and remove the pits. Scoop out a little of the pulp to enlarge hollow. Mash the pulp.

Cream the butter and sugar together; mix in the crumbs, peach pulp, egg yolk, and cognac. Stuff the peaches. Arrange in a buttered baking dish and sprinkle 1 teaspoon of wine on each. Pour the water into the dish. Bake in a 350° oven 25 minutes or until tender but still firm.

Serves 6.

PERE COTTE ROSSE

Baked Pears in Red Wine

8 firm pears	½ teaspoon grated lemon rind
1⅛ cups sugar	4 cups dry red wine

Peel the pears, but leave stem on. Mix together the sugar, lemon rind, and wine in a baking dish. Place the pears in it. Cover dish and bake in a 350° oven 50 minutes or until pears are tender but firm. Baste and turn pears frequently. Chill.

Serves 8.

Note: White wine may be substituted for the red, in which case the dish is called Pere Cotte Bianche.

CREMA d'ANANAS

Pineapple Parfaits

6 egg yolks	⅓ cup cognac
½ cup sugar	2 cups heavy cream
½ cup crushed drained canned pineapple	

Beat the egg yolks and sugar in the top of a double boiler. Place over hot water and cook, stirring constantly, until thick and frothy. Remove from heat and stir in the cognac. Chill 2 hours.

Whip the cream and fold into the yolk mixture with the pineapple. Spoon into 8-10 parfait glasses or sherbet cups. Chill 2 hours before serving.

Serves 8-10.

OMELETTE alla FIAMA

Apricot Dessert Omelet

4 egg yolks	2 tablespoons confectioners' sugar
¼ teaspoon salt	
4 egg whites, stiffly beaten	4 tablespoons warm cognac
3 tablespoons butter	

Beat the egg yolks and salt until light. Fold in the egg whites. Melt the butter in a 9- or 10-inch skillet; pour in the egg mixture. Cook over low heat until bottom is delicately browned. Bake in a preheated 400° oven 5 minutes or until set and top browned. Spread with jam. Roll up onto a heated serving dish. Sprinkle with the sugar. Place under the broiler to glaze.

Pour the cognac over the omelet and set aflame.

Serves 3-4.

ARANCI CARAMELLIZZATI

Oranges in Syrup

6 oranges	1½ cups sugar
	¾ cup water

Wash the oranges and very carefully peel them. Scrape the inside of the peel to remove any white part and cut the peel (of 3 oranges) into julienne pieces. Cook in boiling water 5 minutes. Drain and reserve.

Cook the sugar and ¾ cup water until thick and syrupy. Turn 1 orange at a time in it to coat all sides. Drain and arrange on a serving dish. Cook the parboiled orange rind in the remaining syrup until transparant and caramel colored. Arrange on top of the oranges. Chill.

Serves 6.

CREMA di MASCHERPONE

Chilled Cheese Dessert

1 pound cream cheese	2 tablespoons heavy cream
½ cup sugar	2 tablespoons cognac
4 egg yolks, beaten	Raspberries or strawberries

Run the cheese in an electric blender or until very smooth or force through a sieve. Beat in the sugar, egg yolks, cream, and cognac, beating until very smooth and thick. Pour into a serving dish and chill. Garnish with raspberries or strawberries.

ZABAGLIONE

Marsala Custard

8 egg yolks	½ cup fine granulated sugar
1 egg white	1 cup Marsala or sweet sherry

In the top of a double boiler, beat the egg yolks, egg white, and sugar with a rotary beater until thick. Beat in the wine; place over hot water and beat until hot and very thick, but do not let boil. Spoon into tall glasses or sherbet cups and serve immediately.

Serves 6-8.

GELATO di MANDORLE

Almond Cream Mold

2 eggs	⅛ teaspoon salt
1 tablespoon corn starch	2 teaspoons almond extract
3 cups light cream	½ cup blanched chopped almonds
½ cup sugar	

Beat the eggs in the top of a double boiler. Mix in the corn starch, then the cream, sugar, and salt. Place over hot water and cook, stirring constantly until thickened, but do not let boil. Stir in the almond extract; strain. Cool, then mix in the almonds. Turn into a buttered melon mold. Place a piece of buttered waxed paper over the top, then cover mold. Place in freezer section of the refrigerator or home freezer. Freeze 4 hours or until firm. To unmold, hold a hot towel around the mold, then turn out onto a chilled serving dish.

Serves 6-8.

BUDIMO di RICOTTA

Cheese-Almond Pudding

1 pound ricotta cheese or
 ½ pound cream cheese and
 ½ pound cottage cheese
5 egg yolks
⅞ cup sugar
⅔ cup ground blanched almonds
⅓ cup chopped candied orange peel
2 teaspoons grated lemon rind

Run the cheese in an electric blender until smooth or force through a sieve. Beat the egg yolks and sugar until light, then beat in the cheese, almonds, orange peel, and lemon rind. Turn into a buttered 7-inch spring form. Bake in a preheated 325° oven 45 minutes. Cool thoroughly before removing from spring-form.

Serves 6-8.

PANNETTONE

Milanese Fruit Bread

2½ cups sifted flour	¼ cup candied fruit, diced
½ teaspoon salt	¼ cup seedless raisins
1 cake or package yeast	2 tablespoons candied citrons, diced
¼ cup lukewarm water	
¼ pound (1 stick) butter	1 tablespoon grated lemon rind
½ cup sugar	
2 eggs	1 egg yolk, beaten
⅓ cup milk, scalded and cooled	

Sift together the flour and salt. Soften the yeast in the water 5 minutes.

Cream the butter and sugar together until light and fluffy. Beat in the eggs, then the yeast mixture. Work in the flour, and just enough of the milk to make a soft dough. Turn out onto a floured surface and knead until smooth. Place in a greased bowl, cover with a towel and let rise in a warm place until double in bulk, about 1 hour.

Turn out onto a floured surface, punch down and knead for a few minutes. Return to bowl, cover and let rise again. Roll out the dough and sprinkle the candied fruit, raisins, citron, and lemon rind over it. Fold over in half and roll gently a couple of times. Form into a loaf and place in a 12-inch greased loaf pan. Cover and let rise for 1 hour. Brush top with the egg yolk. Bake in a preheated 350° oven 45 minutes or until browned and shrunk away from the sides of the pan. Cool on a cake rack.

PANAFORTE di SIENA

Nougat

- 1 cup sifted flour
- ¼ cup unsweetened cocoa
- 2 teaspoons cinnamon
- ¼ teaspoon ground allspice
- 1 cup honey
- 1 cup sugar
- 1 pound candied fruit, finely diced
- ½ pound shelled almonds, toasted
- ½ pound shelled filberts (hazel nuts) toasted
- 2 tablespoons grated orange rind
- Confectioners' sugar

Sift together the flour, cocoa, cinnamon, and allspice. Combine the honey and sugar in a saucepan, cook over low heat, stirring constantly with a wooden spoon for 10 minutes. Remove from the heat; blend in the flour mixture, then the candied fruit, almonds, filberts, and orange rind. Turn into a greased 8-by 12-inch pan evenly. Bake in a preheated 275° oven 45 minutes or until firm. Sift confectioners' sugar over the top and return to the oven for 2 minutes. Cool on a cake rack, sprinkle top again with confectioners' sugar. Cut into 1-inch squares. When cold, wrap individual pieces in foil or waxed paper and store in an airtight container. Keeps indefinitely.

INDEX

Index

A

Abbacchio, 18
  (alla) Cacciatora, 105-106
  (al) Forno, 104
  Marinato, 104-105
  Pasticciare, 107
  (ai) Piselli, 105
  Sbrodettato, 106
Acqua del Serino (wine), 27
Agnello, Costatelle d', 107-108
Agnolotti, 15
Albana di Romagna (wine), 24-25
Aleatico del Viterbese (wine), 27
Alfredo (all'), fettucini, 69
Almond(s):
  -cheese pudding, 152
  cream mold, 151-152
Amaretti, 145-146
Amatriciana (all'), spaghetti, 68
Anchovy(ies):
  Bagna Cauda, 32
  (and) cheese appetizer, 36-37
  dip (hot), for raw vegetables, 32
  Spiedini alla Romana, 36-37
Animelle alla Ciociara, 123-124
Anitra all'Olive, 95
Anitra in Agrodolce, 96
Antipasto, 20
  Fagioli alla Toscana, 131
  (di) Funghi e Pomodori, 34
  See also Appetizers

Appetizer(s), 32-37
  anchovy dip (hot), for raw vegetables, 32
  Antipasto di Funghi e Pomodori, 34
  Bagna Cauda, 32
  bean (white) and tuna fish, 35
  beans (white) and caviar, 35
  cheese and anchovy, 36-37
  cheese sticks, fried, 37
  cheese-stuffed mushrooms, 36
  chicken liver pâté on toast, 32-33
  Crostini di Fegato, 32-33
  Crostini di Pomodori, 33
  Fagioli con Caviale, 35
  Fagioli Toscani col Tonno, 35
  Funghi alla Parmigiana, 36
  Insalata di Scampi e Funghi, 34
  Mozzarella alla Milanese, 37
  mushroom and tomato, 34
  Peperoni alla Piemontese, 33-34
  pepper appetizer, 33-34
  shrimp and mushroom, 34
  Spiedini alla Romana, 36-37
  tomato canapés, 33
  vegetables (raw), hot anchovy dip for, 32
Apricot dessert omelet, 150
Aragosta all'Ambasciatori, 53

157

158 / Index

Aragosta alla Griglia, 52
Aranci Caramellizzati, 150-151
Arista alla Fiorentina, 108
Artichokes:
    Roman-style, 129
    Scaloppine al Carciofi, 110-111
    (and) veal, 110-111
    (in) vegetable omelet, 60
Asiago (cheese), 29-30
Asparagi Parmigiana, 129-130
Asparagus, 17
    Lombatina con Verdure, 112-113
    (with) Parmesan cheese, 129-130
    soup, cream of, 43-44
    Tacchino (Filetto di) con Formaggio, 93-94
    (in) turkey rolls, 93-94
    (in) veal chops with vegetables, 112-113
    Zuppa di Asparagi, 43-44
Assisi, 18
Asti Spumante (wine), 21

B

Baccalà mantecato, 12
Bacon:
    sauce for spaghetti, 68
    Spaghetti all'Amatriciana, 68
Bagna Cauda, 12, 15, 32
Barbaresco (wine), 21
Barbera (wine), 21
Bardolino (wine), 24
Barolo (wine), 21
Battelmatt (cheese), 29
Bazzotto (cheese), 29
Bean(s), use of, 17
Bean(s)—green:
    Fagiolini al Prosciutto, 130
    Fritto Misto, 127-128
    (with) ham, 130
    Italian-style, 130-131
    (in) mixed fried foods, 127-128
Bean(s)—lima
    Fagioli en Salsa, 131
    Fave Fresche Stufato, 132
    (with) ham, 132
    Italian style, 131
Bean(s)—red, baked, 132
Bean(s)—white:
    (and) caviar appetizer, 35
    Fagioli alla Toscana, 131
    Fagioli con Caviale, 35
    Fagioli Toscani col Tonno, 35
    Minestrone alla Genovese, 41
    Minestrone alla Milanese, 40-41
    (and) rice soup, 42
    (and) tuna fish appetizer, 35
    soup, Tuscan style, 42-43
    Tuscan style, 131
    (in) vegetable soup, pureed, 39-40
    Zuppa alla Veneziana, 39-40

Index / 159

Zuppa di Fagioli alla Tuscana, 42-43
Zuppa di Fagioli e Riso, 42

Beef:
- Bollito Misto, 128
- braised, in red wine, 103-104
- Bue alla Moda del Lombardia, 102-103
- Costa di Manzo al Vino Rosso, 101
- Filetto al Pâté, 99-100
- Filetto al Vermouth, 99
- Filetto Ripieno, 100
- fillets, stuffed, 100
- fillet, with Pâté, 99-100
- fillet, with vermouth sauce, 99
- Manzo Brasato, 103-104
- Manzo Ripieno, 100-101
- marinated roast, 101
- Ragu, 83
- ravioli, 74
- rice soup, 43
- roast, 101
- soup, with eggs, 38
- (in) spicy sauce, 102
- Stufatino alla Romana, 102
- Stufato di Manzo alla Genovese, 103
- stuffed, 100-101
- stew, Roman style, 102
- Sugo di Carne, 81-82
- Tacchino Ripieno, 94-95
- Trippa alla Fiorentina, 126-127
- vegetable soup, puréed, 39

(with) white wine, 103
Zucchini Ripiene, 139
Zuppa alla Pavese, 38
Bel Paese (cheese), 27, 28, 64, 137
Bel Paesino (cheese), 28 102-103
Budimo di Ricotta, 152
Butter, cookery use of, 15
Bell peppers *See* Peppers
Bergamo, 28
Bianco di Portofino (wine), 22
Biscuit Tortoni, 143
Bistecca alla Fiorentina, 9, 17
"Blue" cheeses, 27-28
Bologna (*alla Bolognese*), 16-17, 24
  breast of chicken (or turkey) and ham, 89
  sauce, 67, 83
Bolognese sauce, 67, 83
Bollito Misto, 128
Bolzano, 14, 22-23
Brachetto d'Asti (wine), 21
Braciole di Vitello Ripieno, 119-120
Bracioline di Maiale al Pomodoro, 108-109
Bracioline di Maiale alla Toscana, 109-110
Braciolette Ripiene, 116-117
Brains. *See* Calf's brains
Broccoli, 17
Brodetto, 14, 18
Brolio (wine), 26
Bue alla Moda del Lombardia,

C

Cacciatora (alla), 18
  eggs, 62
  lamb, 105-106
Cacciucco, 17
Cacciucco alla Fiorentina, 51-52
Caciofiore (cheese), 30
Caciotte (cheese), 30
Cake(s):
  Certosina, 144-145
  chestnut refrigerator tart, 148
  Gato di Castagne, 148
  Pane di Spugna, 145
  Pannettone, 153
  spice-nut, 144-145
  sponge, 145
Caldaro (wine), 23
Calf's brains:
  Crocchette di Cervella, 124
  croquettes, 124
  Fritto Misto (fried), 127-128
Calf's liver:
  breaded, 125
  Fritto Misto (fried), 127-128
  (in) Marsala, 124-125
Calvenzano (cheese), 28
Campagnola (alla), spaghettini, 69
Canapés See Appetizers
Cannelloni (cheese-stuffed noodles), 66
Cannelloni (egg pasta), 66
  egg dough for, 65
Capelletti (pasta), 17
Capers, 32, 120, 141

Caper sauce, 92-93
Capon, roast, with caper sauce, 92-93
Cappone Arrosto, 92-93
Carciofi. See Artichoke(s)
Carema (wine), 21
Carmignano (wine), 26
Carrots:
  Carote Agrodolce, 133
  sweet and sour, 133
Carsenza (cheese), 30
Casserole(s):
  lamb, 107
  sweetbreads and chicken livers, 98
Casoeula, 110
Castelli Romani (wine), 26-27
Castelmagno (cheese), 28
Cauliflower:
  Cavolfiore alla Milanese, 133
  (with) cheese, 133
  Fritto Misto (fried), 127-128
Caviar:
  (and) beans (white), appetizer, 35
  Fagioli con Caviale, 35
Cavolfiore alla Milanese, 133
Celery:
  Parmigiana, 134
  Sedano Parmigiana, 134
Cenci, 146
Certosina (cake), 144-145
Certosino (cheese), 30
Cesane del Piglio (wine), 27

Index / 161

Cheese(s), 27-30, 59-64
-almond pudding, 152
(and) anchovy appetizer, 36-37
cauliflower with, 133
Cavolfiore alla Milanese, 133
cheese-stuffed mushrooms, 36
corn meal and, 80-81
Costolette di Vitello con Formaggio, 114
dessert, chilled, 151
(and) eggplant, baked, 134-135
noodles (egg) with butter and cheese sauce, 69
omelets, 59
(and) potato croquettes, 137-138
sauce, chicken breasts with, 88
sticks, fried, 37
Tacchino (Filetto di) con Formaggio, 93-94
-truffle fondue, 64
turkey rolls, 93-94
veal with, 114
See also Bel Paese; Cottage Cheese; Cream Cheese; Gruyère; Mozzarella; Parmesan; Romano; Swiss

Chestnut(s):
dessert, 147
dessert, frozen, 147-148
Gato di Castagne, 148
Monte Bianco, 147
Plombières, 147-148
refrigerator tarte, 148
soup, 44
Tacchino Ripieno, 94-95
(in) turkey stuffing, 94-95
Zuppa di Castagne, 44

Chianti (wine), 19, 25-26
Chiaretto (wine), 22

Chicken:
(in) boiled mixed meats, 128
breasts, and ham, 89
breasts, in cheese sauce, 88
breasts, Milan style, 88-89
broiled, deviled, 86
deviled, broiled, 86
Florence style, 85
fricassee, 89, 97
fried, marinated, 85-86
fried, mixed, 127-128
Fritto Misto, 127-128
-ham croquettes, 93
pancakes, stuffed, filling for, 63
(and) peppers, Umbrian style, 90
Piedmont style, 85
ravioli, 74
rice soup, 43
roast stuffed, 91
Roman style, 86-87
Roman style, with peppers, 92
stuffing, 91
See also Chicken livers; Pollo

Chicken livers:
beef, stuffed, 100-101
Bolognese sauce(s), 83
chicken liver pâté on toast, 32-33
chicken liver sauce, 84
Crostini di Fegato, 32-33
eggs, hunter's style, 62
Manzo Ripieno, 100-101
noodle soup, Milan style, 39
noodles (broad) with tomato-meat sauce, 72-73
Pappardelle alla Toscana, 72-73
Pasta in Brodo con Fegatini, 39
pâté on toast, 32

162 / Index

Piccioni con Piselli, 96-97
Ragu, 83
rice (special) dish, 79
Risotto Speciale, 79
Salsa di Fegatini, 84
Scaloppine al Fegato, 123
squab with peas, 96-97
sweetbreads and chicken liver casserole, 98
Tegamino, 98
Uova alla Cacciatora, 62
(with) veal, 123
(in) wine sauce, 87
Ciclio (cheese), 30
Cinque Terre (wine), 22
Clam juice, 49, 54
Clam sauces, 70-71
Coffee ice cream, 143
Colli Euganei (wine), 24
Corn meal:
  (and) cheese, 80-81
  Paparot, 45
  pie, 80
  -spinach soup, 45
  See also Polenta
Coronata (wine), 22
Cortese dell'Alto (wine), 21
Costa di Manzo al Vino Rosso, 101
Costatelle d'Agnello, 107-108
Costatelle di Maiale alla Milanese, 109
Costatelle alla Milanese, 15
Costolette di Pollo, 88
Costolette di Vitello con Formaggio, 114
Cottage cheese, uses for, 76, 118, 152
Cozze alla Marinara, 53-54
Cream cheese, uses for, 115, 118, 152
Crema d'Ananas, 149-150
Crema di Mascherpone, 151
Cremini (cheese), 30
Cremona, 30
Crescenza (cheese), 30
Crescenza Lombardi (cheese), 30
Crisps (fried), 146
Crocchette di Cervella, 124
Crocchette di Patate, 137-138
Crocchette di Pollo con Prosciutto, 93
Croquettes:
  calf's brains, 124
  chicken-ham, 93
  potato-cheese, 137-138
Crostini di Fegato, 32-33
Crostini di Pomodori, 33
Crullers, 146-147
Custard, Marsala, 151

D

Dessert(s), 143-154
  almond cream mold, 151-152
  Amaretti, 145-146
  apricot dessert omelet, 150
  Aranci Caramellizzati, 150-151
  Biscuit Tortoni, 143
  Budimo di Ricotta, 152
  Cenci, 146
  Certosina, 144-145
  cheese-almond pudding, 152
  cheese dessert, chilled, 151

chestnut dessert, 147
chestnut dessert, frozen, 147-148
chestnut refrigerator tart, 148
coffee ice cream, 143
Crema d'Ananas, 149-150
Crema di Mascherpone, 151
crullers, 146-147
fried crisps, 146
fruit bread, Milan style, 153
Gato di Castagne, 148
Gelato di Caffe, 143
Gelato di Fragole, 144
Gelato di Mandorle, 151-152
macaroons, 145-146
Marsala custard, 151
Monte Bianco, 147
nougat, 154
Omelette alla Fiama, 150
oranges in syrup, 150-151
Panaforte di Siena, 154
Pane di Spugna, 145
Pannettone, 153
peaches, stuffed and baked, 148-149

pears baked in red wine, 149
Pere Cotte Rosse, 149
Pesche Ripiene, 148-149
pineapple parfaits, 149-150
Plombieres di Castagne, 147-148
Sfinge, 146-147
spice-nut cake, 144-145
sponge cake, 145
strawberry ice cream, 144
Zabaglioni, 151
Dolce Verde (cheese), 28
Dolceacqua (region), 22
Dolcetto delle Langhe (wine), 21
Duck
 (with) olive sauce, 85
 (in) sweet and sour sauce, 96
Dumplings:
 potato, 75-76
 semolina, 75
 spinach-cheese, 76

E

Egg(s), 59-64
 apricot dessert omelet, 150
 baked in potato nests, 61
 beef soup with, 38
 (and) cheese, 59-63
 cheese omelet, 59
 cheese-truffle fondue, 64
 dough, 65
 egg-ribbon soup, 38
 hunter's style, 62
 Parma style, 62
 pasta, 66, 74
 sauce, 72, 106

 (and) spinach, 61
 spinach pancake omelet, 59-60
 vegetable omelet, 60
Egg sauce:
 lamb in, 106
 noodles with, 72
Eggplant:
 (and) cheese, baked, 134
 Fritto Misto (fried), 127-128
 (in) lamb casserole, 107
 (in) Minestrone, 41
 stuffed, 135

164 / Index

Elba (island), wine, 26
Emilia-Romagna, 16-17, 24, 29, 30
Emiliano (cheese), 29
Erbo (cheese), 28
Est! Est! Est!!! (wine), 27

F

Fagioli all'Uccelletto, 17
   alla Toscana, 131
   con Caviale, 35
   en Salsa, 131
   Toscani col Tonno, 35
Fagiolini all'Italiana, 130-131
Fasoeil al Forno, 132
Fave Fresche Stufato, 132
Fegatini di Pollo, 87
Fegato, scaloppine al, 123
Fegato alla Veneziana, 11, 14
   di Vitello al Marsala, 124-125
   di Vitello alla Milanese, 125
Fettucini, 16
   (all') Alfredo, 69
   egg dough for, 65
   (alla) Papalina, 72
   (alla) Romana, 18
Fiasco (covering), 26
Filetto al Pâté, 99-100
   al Vermouth, 99
   di Pollo alla Bolognese, 89
   Ripieno, 100
Fior d'Alpe (cheese), 28, 30
Fiorentina (alla). *See* Florence
Fish, 49-58
   Cacciucco alla Fiorentina, 51-52
   (with) mushroom-wine sauce, 50-51
   Pesce alla Romana, 50-51
   soup, 47-48
   stew, 51-52
   Zuppa di Pesce alla Veneziana, 47-48
Florence (*alla Fiorentina*), 9, 12, 17
   chicken, fried, marinated, 85-86
   eggs and spinach, 61
   fish stew, 51-52
   peas, 135-136
   pork roast, 108
   tripe, in meat sauce, 126-127
Fondue, cheese-truffle, 64
Fonduta, 11, 15, 64
Fontina cheese, 15-16, 29
   Fonduta, 64
Formaggio. *See* Cheese
Formaggio dei Pastori (cheese), 30
Frascati (wine), 27
Freisa d'Asti (wine), 21
Fricassee
   chicken, 89-90
   turkey, 97
Fried foods, mixed, 127-128
Fried crisps, 146
Frittata, 60
   al Formaggio, 59
   di Spinaci, 59-60
   Trentina, 15
Frittatine Imboccice, 63
Frittele di Aragosta o Scampi, 57
Fritto Misto, 127-128
Fruit bread. *See* Pannettone
Funghi. *See* Mushrooms
Funghi alla Parmigiana, 36

G

Gamberettini in Crema, 56
Garda (lake), 22, 24
Garda (wine), 22
Garganega di Gambellara (wine), 24
Gato di Castagne, 148
Gattinara (wine), 21
Gelato di Caffè, 143
  di Fragole, 144
  di Mandorle, 151-152
Genoa (*alla Genovese*), 9, 12, 16, 22
  beef with white wine, 103
  meat sauce, 81
  minestrone, 41
  rice, 177
  zucchini, 140
Giacomelli Schiachetra (wine), 22

Gnocchi, 11, 14-15
  chicken liver sauce for, 84
  potato, 75-76
  seminola, 75
  spinach-cheese, 76
Gorgonzola (cheese), 27-28
Grana (Parmesan cheese), 28-29
Green beans. *See* Bean(s)
Green noodles. *See* Noodles
Green peppers. *See* Peppers
Gremolada (sauce), 12
Grignolino d'Asti (wine), 21
Groviera (cheese), 29
Grumello (wine), 22
Gruviera (cheese), 29
Gruyère (cheese), 29
Guncinà (wine), 23

H

Ham:
  Animelle alla Ciociara, 123-124
  (in) Bolognese sauce, 83
  -chicken croquettes, 93
  Crocchette di Pollo con Prosciutto, 93
  Fagiolini al Prosciutto, 130
  Fave Fresche Stufato, 132
  (and) green beans, 130
  lima beans with, 132
  -potato pie, 137
  Role di Vitello, 117-118
  Saltimbocca, 117
  Scaloppine di Vitella al Prosciutto, 115-116
  Scaloppine Ripiene, 116
  Tacchino (Filetto di) con Formaggio, 93-94
  Torta di Patata e Prosciutto, 137
  (in) turkey rolls, 93-94
  Valdostana di Vitello, 115
  (with) veal, 115-116

166 / Index

(and) veal, Milan style, 115
(and) veal, rolled, 117-118
(and) veal rolls, 117, 118
(and) veal rolls, stuffed, 116-117
Ham sauce, 70

I

Ice cream:
  coffee, 143
  Gelato di Caffè, 143
  Gelato di Fragole, 144
  strawberry, 144
Inferno (wine), 22
Insalata
  (di) Cipolla, 142
  (di) Riso, 141-142

(di) Scampi e Funghi, 34
Verde, 141
Involtini di Vitello, 118
Involto di Vitello alla Milanese, 114-115
Iota alla Triestina (soup), 12
Italian - American restaurants, 11, 25
Italian Riviera, 16, 21-22

K

Kidneys:
  braised, 125-126
  Rognoni al Vino Bianco, 126

Rognoni Trifolati, 125-126
(in) white wine, 126

L

Lagrein Rosato (wine), 23
Lamb:
  Abbacchio ai Piselli, 105
  al Forno, 104
  alla Cacciatora, 105-106
  Marinato, 104-105
  Pasticciare, 107
  Sbrodettato, 106
  braised, with peas, 105
  casserole, 107

chops, in white wine, 107-108
Costatelle d'Agnello, 107-108
(in) egg sauce, 106
fell (skin), 104
hunter's style, 105-106
marinated roast, 104-105
roast leg of, 104-105
Lambrusco (wine), 24
Lasagne, 18
  egg dough for, 65

Lasagne Verde alla Bolognese, 17, 66-67
Latium, 14, 18, 26
Lentil soup, 46
Liguria, 16, 20-22
Lima beans. *See* Bean(s)
Liver:
  breaded, 125
  Fritto Misto (fried), 127-128
  (in) Marsala, 124
  See also Chicken livers

Lobster:
  Aragosta all'Ambasciatori, 53
  alla Griglia, 52
  broiled, 52
  fried, 57-58
  Frittele di Aragosta, 57-58
  (in) liquor sauce, 53
Lodi, 28
Lomatine al Cartoccio, 113
Lombardy, 12, 15, 22, 29, 30, 102-103
Lombatina con Verdure, 112-113

M

Macaroons, 145-146, 148-149
Maiale:
  Arist alla Fiorentina, 108
  bracioline, al pomodoro, 108-109
  bracioline, alla Toscana, 109-110
  casoeula, 110
  costolette, alla Milanese, 109
Malvasia di Grottaferrata (wine), 27
Manzo (Stufato di) alla Genovese, 103
  Brasato, 103-104
  Ripieno, 100-101
Marches, 17-18, 25, 29, 30
Marsala (wine):
  custard, 151
  recipes using, 77, 79, 84, 87, 93, 99, 108, 112, 116-117, 119, 121, 124-125, 148, 151
Marzemino (wine), 23
Mascarpone (cheese), 30

Meat(s)
  See also Beef; Ham; Lamb; Pork; Prosciutto; Sausage; Veal
Meat sauce(s), 81-82
  (for) tripe, 126-127
Melenzana alla Parmigiana, 134-135
  Ripiene, 135
Meranese di Collina (wine), 23
Milan (*alla Milanese*), 12, 13, 15, 22
  calf's liver, 125
  cauliflower with cheese, 133
  cheese sticks, 37
  chicken breasts, 88
  fruit bread, 153
  minestrone, 40-41
  noodle soup, 39
  Pannettone, 153
  pork chops, 109
  veal and ham, 115
  veal rolls, 114-115
Minestra di Lenticchie, 46

168 / Index

Minestrina di Riso, 43
Minestrone alla Genovese, 41
   alla Milanese, 40-41
Mixed fried foods, 127-128
Monferrato (wine), 21
Mont Blanc. *See* Monte Bianco
Montalbano (wine), 26
Monte Bianco, 147
Montecarlo (wine), 26
Montefiascone, 27
Montepulciano, Vin Nobile de (wine), 26
Mortadella (sausage), 17
Moscat di Terracina (wine), 27
Moscato d'Asti (wine), 21
Moscato di Casteggio (wine), 22
Mozzarella (cheese), recipes using, 30, 36-37, 61, 64, 66, 93-94, 100, 114, 119-120, 134-135
Mushroom(s):
   Animelle alla Ciociara, 123-124
   Antipasto di Funghi e Pomodori, 34
   cheese-stuffed, appetizer, 36
   fish with mushroom-wine sauce, 50-51
   Frittata, 60
   Funghi alla Parmigiana, 36
   Insalata di Scampi e Funghi, 34
   (and) shrimp appetizer, 34
   Spaghetti alla Campagnola, 69
   spaghetti with mushrooms and anchovies, 69
   (and) sweetbreads and ham, 123-124
   (and) tomato appetizer, 34
Mushroom(s)—dried:
   broad-noodles with tomato-meat sauce, 72-73
   meat sauces, 81-82
   Minestrone alla Genovese, 41
   Pappardelle alla Toscana, 72-73
   Sugo di Carne, 81-82
Mussel(s):
   alla Marinara, 53-54
   (in) wine, 53-54

N

Naples (Neopolitans), 10-12, 18
Nebbiolo Piemontese (wine), 21
Noodle(s):
   butter and cheese sauce, 69
   Cannelloni, 66
   cheese-stuffed, 66
   egg sauce, 72
   Fettucini all'Alfredo, 69
   Fettucini alla Papalina, 72
   green, 67
   Lasagna Verde alla Bolognese, 67
   Pappardelle alla Toscana, 72-73
   Pasta in Brodo con Fegatini, 39
   Polpette al Pomodoro, 121
   soufflé, 73
   soup, Milan style, 39

Index / 169

tomato-meat sauce, 72-73
veal and zucchini casserole, 121
vegetable soup, puréed, 39

Zuppa alla Veneziana, 39
Nougat, 154
Nutmeg, uses of, 45, 75, 76, 83, 114, 122, 137, 144

O

Olive(s), recipes using, 95, 99, 136-137, 141-142
Olive oil, use of, 15, 17
Omelet(s):
 apricot dessert, 150
 cheese, 59
 spinach pancake, 59-60
 vegetable, 60

Omelette alla Fiama, 150
Onion salad, 142
Oranges in syrup, 150-151
Oregano, recipes using, 36, 39, 100, 139
Orvieto (wine), 18, 25, 26
Ossi buchi, 15, 112

P

Padua, 13
Panaforte di Siena, 154
Pancake(s), stuffed, 63
Pane di Spugna, 145
Pannettone, 153
Papalina (alla), fettucini, 72
Paparot (soup), 45
Pappardelle (noodles), 17
Pappardelle alla Toscana, 72-73
Parfait, pineapple, 149-150
Pasta(s), 11-13, 15-17, 19-20, 65-84
 (and) sauces, 65-84
Pasta al Uovo, 65
 in Brodo con Fegatini, 39
Passiti (wine), 26
Pastorella (cheese), 28
Pâté de foie gras, 99

Pavia (*alla Pavese*), 38
Pea(s):
 Abbacchio ai Piselli, 105
 Florence style, 135-136
 lamb, braised, with peas, 105
 Lombatina con Verdure, 112-113
 Piccioni con Piselli, 96-97
 (and) rice, 77
 Risi e Bisi, 77
Peaches, stuffed baked, 148-149
Pears, in red wine, baked, 149
Pecorino (cheese), 29
Pecorino Romano (cheese), 29
Peperoni alla Piemontese, 33-34
 alla Romana, 136
 Ripieno, 136-137

170 / Index

Peppers (bell)—green and red:
  Abbacchio Pasticciare, 107
  appetizer, 33-34
  chicken, Roman style, 91-92
  (and) chicken, Umbrian style, 90
  (in) lamb casserole, 107
  Peperoni alla Piemontese, 33-34
  Peperoni alla Romana, 136
  Peperoni Ripieno, 136-137
  Pollo alla Romana, 91-92
  Pollo Novello e Peperoni, 90
  Roman style, 136
  Spezzatino di Vitello, 122
  stuffed, 136-137
  (in) veal stew, 122
Pere Cotte Rosse, 149
Perugia, 12, 18, 26
Pesce alla Romana, 50-51
Pesche Ripiene, 148-149
Pesto sauce, 12, 16
Petti di Pollo al Prosciutto, 88-89
Piccate al Marsala, 119
Piccioni con Piselli, 96-97
Piceno Rosso (wine), 25
Piedmont district (*alla Piemontese*), 15, 21-22, 33, 85
Pineapple parfait, 149-150
Pisa, 12, 17
Piselli alla Fiorentina, 135-136
Plombières di Castagne, 147-148
Polcevera (wine), 22
Polenta, 12, 14-16
  (al) Formaggio, 80-81
  Pasticciata, 80
Pollo:
  Arrosto, 91
  (alla) Bolognese, 89
  Costolette di, 88
  (alla) Piemontese, 85
  Crocchette, con Prosciutto, 93
  (alla) Diavolo, 86
  Fegatini di, 87
  Filetto di, alla Bolognese, 89
  Filetto di, con Formaggio, 93-94
  (alla) Fiorentina, 85-86
  Fricasse di, 89-90
  Novello e Peperoni, 90
  Petti di, al Prosciutto, 88-89
  (alla) Romana, 86-87, 91-92
Polpette al Pomodoro, 121
Polpettine di Vitello, 121-122
Pomodori Gratinati, 138
  Ripieni, 138-139
Pomidoro. *See* Tomato(es)
Pomino (wine), 26
Pork:
  Arista alla Fiorentina, 108
  Bracioline di Maiale al Pomodoro, 108-109
  Bracioline di Maiale alla Toscana, 109-110
  Casoeula, 110
  casserole, 110
  chops, braised, 109-110
  chops, breaded, 109
  chops, in tomato sauce, 108-109
  Costatelle di Maiale alla Milanese, 109
  roast, Florence style, 108
Potato(es):
  —cheese croquettes, 137-138
  Crocchette di Patate, 137-138
  dumplings, 75-76
  eggs baked in potato nests, 61
  Gnocchi di Patate, 75-76
  —ham pie, 137
  Torta di Patata e Prosciutto, 137
  Tortina d'Uova, 61

Index / 171

—vegetable soup, 47
Zuppa di Verdure, 47
Poultry, 85-98
See also Capon; Chicken;
Duck; Squab; Turkey
Procanico (wine), 26
Prosciutto
Petti di Pollo al, 88-89

Scaloppine di Vitella al, 115-116
Torta di Patata e, 137
See also Ham
Prosecco di Conegliano (wine), 24
Provolone (cheese), 30

R

Ragu (sauce), 17, 83
Raspberry chilled cheese dessert, 151
Ravioli, 15, 16, 74
Recioto Veronese (wine), 24
Red peppers. See Peppers
Restaurants, 10-11, 25
Rice:
(and) bean soup, 42
Genoa style, 77
green, 78
Insalata di Riso, 141-142
Minestrina di Riso, 43
Ossi buchi, 112
(and) peas, 77
Risi e Bisi, 77
Riso Verde, 78
Risotto Speciale, 79
soup, 43
special rice dish, 79
(and) vegetable salad, 141-142
Zuppa di Fagioli e Riso, 42

Ricotta (cheese), 29, 66, 76, 118, 152
Ricotta Salata (cheese), 29
Risi e Bisi, 14, 77
Riso alla Genovese, 77-78
Riso Verde, 78
Risotto, 12, 13, 15
Ossi buchi, 112
(di) Scampi, 57
Speciale, 79
Riviera del Garda (wine), 22
Robiola (cheese), 28
Robiolina (cheese), 28
Rognoni al Vino Bianco, 126
Rognoni Trifolati, 125-126
Role di Vitello, 117-118
Romano (cheese), 29, 38, 42, 75, 90
Roquefort (cheese), 27-28
Rosés, 19, 24
Rossara (wine), 23
Rossese (wine), 22
Rosso Piceno (wine), 25
Rufina (wine), 26

S

Saffron, 15, 47
Salad(s), 141-142
Salerno, 12
Salsa alla Genovese, 81
   di Fegatini, 84
   di Pomodoro, 84
Saltimbocca, 117
Sangiovese di Romagna (wine), 24
Santa Guistina (wine), 23
Santa Madalena (wine), 23
Sardinia, 29
Sassella (wine), 22
Sauce(s), 65-84
   bacon, for spaghetti, 68
   béarnaise, 128
   (for) Bollito Misto, 128
   Bolognese, 67, 83
   butter and cheese, 69
   caper, for roast capon, 92-93
   cheese, for chicken breasts, 88
   clam (red), for spaghetti, 70
   clam (white), for spaghetti, 71
   egg, for lamb, 106
   egg, for noodles, 72
   green, for zucchini, 140
   gremolada, 12
   ham, for spaghetti, 70
   meat, 81-82
   meat, for tripe, 126-127
   meat, Genoa style, 81
   meat-tomato, for noodles, 72-73
   mushroom and anchovy, for spaghettini, 69
   mustard, 128
   olive sauce, for duck, 95
   pesto, 12, 16
   spicy, for beef, 102-103
   sweet and sour, for carrots, 133
   sweet and sour, for duck, 96
   tomato, 84, 128
   tomato, for pork chops, 108
   tomato, for veal balls, 121
   tomato-meat, for noodles, 72-73
   truffle, for spaghetti, 68
   tuna fish, for veal, 121
   vermouth, for fillet of beef, 99
   wine, for chicken livers, 87
Sausage(s), 18, 94-95, 128
Sbrinz (cheese), 30
Scaloppine al Carciofi, 110-111
   al Fegato, 123
   di Vitella al Prosciutto, 115-116
   Ripiene, 116
Scampi:
   Frittele di, 57-58
   Fritti, 58
   Gamberitti in Crema, 56
   (alla) Lago di Como, 54
   (alla) Marinara, 55
   Risotto di, 57
   (alla) Spiedo, 55-56
Schiave (wine), 23
Seafood, 12-14, 16-18, 20, 24-25
   see also Lobster; Mussels; Shrimp; Sole

Sedano Parmigiana, 134
Semolina dumplings, 75
Sfinge, 146-147
Sformato di Vitello, 122
Sherry (wine), recipes using, 77, 79, 84, 87, 93, 99, 108, 112, 116, 117, 119, 121, 124, 148, 151
Shrimp(s):
  (in) cream, 56
  fisherman's style, 55
  fried, 57-58
  Lake Como style, 54
  (and) mushroom appetizer, 34
  Risotto, 57
  (on) skewers, 55
Sicily, 10, 11, 18, 20
Siena, 17, 26; Panaforte di, 154
Soave (wine), 23, 25
Sogliole alla Veneziana, 49
  Marinara, 50
Sole
  fisherman's style, 50
  (with) Parmesan cheese, 49
  Sogliole alla Parmigiana, 49-50
  alla Veneziana, 49
  Marinara, 50
  Venetian style, 49
Sorrento, 12
Soufflé
  noodle, 73
  (di) Tagliarini, 73
Soup(s), 38-48
  asparagus, cream of, 43
  bean (white), Tuscan style, 42-43
  bean (white) and rice soup, 42
  beef, with eggs, 38
  chestnut, 44
  egg-ribbon, 38

fish, 47-48
Iota alla Triestina, 12
lentil, 46
Minestra di Lenticchie, 46
Minestrina di Riso, 43
Minestrone alla Genovese, 41
  alla Milanese, 40-41
noodle, Milan style, 39
Paparot, 45
Pasta in Brodo con Fegatini, 39
potato-vegetable, 47
rice, 43
spinach-corn meal, 45
spinach-egg soup, 45
Straciatella alla Romana, 38
tomato, cream of, 46
vegetable, Genoa style, 41
vegetable, Milan style, 40-41
vegetable, puréed, 39-40
vegetable-potato, 47
Zuppa alla Pavese, 38
Zuppa alla Veneziana, 39-40
Zuppa di Asparagi, 43-44
Zuppa di Castagne, 44
Zuppa di Fagioli alla Toscana, 42-43
Zuppa di Fagioli e Riso, 42
Zuppa di Pomidoro, 46
Zuppa di Spinaci, 45
Zuppa di Verdure, 47
Southern Italian style, 11-12, 13
Spaghetti
  (all') Amatriciana, 18, 68
  (with) bacon sauce, 68
  Bolognese sauce, 83
  (alla) Campagnola, 69
  (alla) Carbonara, 70
  chicken liver sauce, 84
  (with) clam (red) sauce, 70
  (with) clam (white) sauce, 71
  (with) ham sauce, 70
  meat sauces, 81-82

174 / Index

(with) mushrooms and anchovies, 69
pesto sauce, 12, 16
(al) Tartufata, 68
tomato sauce, 84
(with) truffle sauce, 68
(alla) Vongole (Bianco), 71
(alla) Vongole (Rosso), 70
Spaghettini, with mushroom and anchovy sauce, 69
Spezzatino di Vitello, 122
Spice-Nut Cake, 144-145
Spicy sauce, 102-103
Spiedini alla Romana, 36-37
Spinach
  Cannelloni, 66
  -cheese dumplings, 76
  corn meal soup, 45
  (and) egg(s), 61
  -egg soup, 45
  Frittata, 59-60
  Gnocchi Verde, 76
  Lasagne Verde alla Bolognese, 67
  -pancake omelet, 59-60
  Paparot, 45
  Riso Verde, 78
  Zuppa di Spinaci, 45

Spoleto, 18
Sponge cake, 145
Spumante d'Elba (wine), 26
Squab, with peas, 96-97
Straciatella alla Romana, 38
Stravecchio (cheese), 29
Stravecchione (cheese), 29
Strawberry(ies):
  chilled cheese dessert, 151
  ice cream, 144
Stufatino alla Romana, 18-19, 102
Stufato di Manzo alla Genovese, 103
Sugo di Carne, 81-82
Sweetbreads:
  Animelle alla Ciociara, 123-124
  (and) chicken liver casserole, 98
  Fritto Misto, 127-128
  (and) ham and mushrooms, 123-124
  (in) mixed fried foods, 127-128
Swiss cheese, 29, 63, 66, 80-81, 88, 93-94, 100, 133, 134, 137

T

Tacchino (Filetto di) alla Bolognese, 89
  con Formaggio, 93-94
  Ripieno, 94-95
  Stufato, 97
Tagliarini. *See* Soufflé
Tagliatelle (egg noodles), 17
Tallegino (cheese), 28
Tallegio (cheese), 28

Tartufi neri, 18
Tegamino, 98
Terlano (wine), 23
Termeno (wine), 23
Teroldego (wine), 23
Tomato(es), 12-13, 17
  Antipasto di Funghi e Pomodori, 34
  baked, 138

Index / 175

canapés, 33
Crostini di Pomodori, 33
meat sauce, for noodles, 72-73
(and) mushroom appetizer, 34
Pappardelle alla Toscana, 72-73
Polpette al Pomodoro, 121
Pomodori Gratinati, 138
Pomodori Ripieni, 138-139
rice-stuffed, 138-139
sauce, for noodles, 72-73
sauce, for pasta, 84
sauce, for pork chops, 108-109
sauce, for tripe, 126-127
sauce, for veal balls, 121
soup, cream of, 46
Zuppa di Pomidoro, 46
Tomato paste, recipes using, 51, 68, 82, 83, 86, 102, 112
Tomato sauce, recipes using, 47, 60, 62, 66, 83, 121, 139
Torta di Patata e Prosciutto, 137
Tortellini (pasta), 17
Tortino d'Uova, 61

Toscano (Vin Santo), 26
Trenette (noodles), 16
Trieste, 12, 13
Tripe, in meat sauce, 126-127
Trippa alla Fiorentina, 17, 126-127
Truffle(s), 18
cheese-truffle fondue, 64
sauce for spaghetti, 68
veal and ham, Milan style, 115
Tuna fish
(and) beans (white), appetizer, 35
Fagioli Toscani col Tonno, 35
Insalata di Riso, 141-142
Peperoni Ripieno, 136-137
(and) rice and vegetable salad, 141-142
stuffed peppers, 136-137
Tuna fish sauce, 120
Turkey
breasts, and ham, 89
fricassee, 97
rolls, 93-94
stuffed, 94-95
Turin, 12, 13, 15

U

Umbria, 18, 26, 30, 90
Uova alla Cacciatora, 62

alla Fiorentina, 61
alla Parmigiana, 62

V

Val d'Aldige (wine), 23
Valdostana di Vitello, 115
Valgella (wine), 22
Valpanena (wine), 24
Valpolicella (wine), 23-24
Valtellina (wine), 22
Veal
  (and) artichokes, 110-111
  balls, in tomato sauce, 121
  boiled mixed meats, 128
  Bollito Misto, 128
  Braciole di Vitello Ripieno, 119-120
  Braciolette Ripiene, 116-117
  calf's liver, in Marsala, 124
  casserole, 122
  (with) cheese, 114
  (with) chicken livers, 123
  chops, in paper, 113
  chops, stuffed, 119-120
  chops, with vegetables, 112-113
  Costolette di Vitello con Formaggio, 114
  country style, 118-119
  croquettes, 121-122
  Fritto Misto, 127-128
  (with) ham, 115-116
  (and) ham, Milan style, 115
  (and) ham, rolled, 117-118
  (and) ham rolls, 117
  Involtini di Vitello, 118
  Involto di Vitello alla Milanese, 114-115
  kidneys, braised, 125-126
  kidneys, in white wine, 126
  Lomatine al Cartoccio, 113
  Lombatina con Verdure, 112-113
  meat sauce, Genoa style, 81
  mixed fried foods, 127
  Ossi buchi, 112
  Piccate al Marsala, 119
  Polpette al Pomodoro, 121
  Polpettine di Vitello, 121-122
  rice, Genoa style, 77-78
  Riso alla Genovese, 77-78
  roast, 111-112
  Rognoni al Vino Bianco, 126
  Rognoni Trifolati, 125-126
  Role di Vitello, 117-118
  rolls, 118
  rolls, ham-stuffed, 116
  rolls, Milan style, 114-115
  Salsa alla Genovese, 81
  Saltimbocca, 117
  scallops, with Marsala, 119
  Scaloppine al Carciofi, 110-111
  Scaloppine al Fegato, 123
  Scaloppine di Vitella al Prosciutto, 115-116
  Scaloppine Ripiene, 116
  Sformato di Vitello, 122
  shins, braised, 112
  stew, 122-123
  Tacchino Ripieno, 94-95
  turkey, stuffing, 94-95
  Valdostana di Vitello, 115
  veal rolls Milanese, 114-115
  Vitello alla Paesana, 118-119
  Vitello Arrosto, 111-112
  Vitello Tonnato, 120
  (and) zucchini casserole, 122

Index / 177

Vegetable(s), 129-140
  Lombatina con Verdure, 112-113
  Minestrone alla Genovese, 41
  Minestrone alla Milanese, 40-41
  omelet, 60—potato soup, 47
  salad with rice, 141-142
  soup, Genoa style, 41
  soup, Milan style, 40-41
  soup, puréed, 39-40
  veal chops with, 112-113
  Zuppa alla Veneziana, 39-40
  Zuppa di Verdure, 47
Venetia (*alla Veneziana*), 13, 22, 23, 24, 29
  vegetable soup, 39
Verdicchio (Dei Castelli di Jesi), wine, 25
Verdiso (wine), 24
Vermentino Ligure (wine), 22
Vermicelli, 39, 41
Vermouth, 56, 86, 99

Vernaccia (wine), 25
Verona, 23-24
Vino alla Veronese (wine), 24
Vitello
  Arrosto, 111-112
  Braciole di, 119
  Costolette, con Formaggio, 114
  Fegato di, al Marsala, 124-125
  Fegato di, alla Milanese, 125
  Involtini di, 118
  Involto, alla Milanese, 114-115
  (alla) Paesana, 118-119
  Polpettine di, 121-122
  Role di, 117-118
  Scaloppine di Vitella al Prosciutto, 115-116
  Sformato di, 122
  Tonnato, 120
  Valdostana di, 115
Vongole. *See* Clam sauces

W

White beans. *See* Beans
Wine(s), 19-27
  dessert, 24, 26, 27
  "roast," 21, 23, 24
  rosé, 22
  sparkling, 20-22, 24
  table, 21
  See also Marsala; Sherry; Vermouth

Z

Zabaione (Zabaglione), 151
Zucchini
  Frittata, 60
  Fritto Misto, 127-128
  (alla) Genovese, 140
  (in) green sauce, 140

178 / Index

(in) Minestrone(s), 41-42
Ripiene, 139
(in) Salsa Verde, 140
sautéed, 140
Sformato di Vitello, 122
stuffed, 139
(and) veal casserole, 122
(in) vegetable omelet, 60
Zuppa alla Pavese, 38
Zuppa alla Veneziana, 39-40

Zuppa di Asparagi, 43-44
Zuppa di Castagne, 44
Zuppa di Fagioli alla Tuscana, 42-43
Zuppa di Fagioli e Riso, 42
Zuppa di Pesce alla Veneziana, 47-48
Zuppa di Pomidoro, 46
Zuppa di Spinaci, 45
Zuppa di Verdure, 47